yOung
Exceptional
children

Monograph Series No. 7

Supporting Early Literacy Development in Young Children

**THE DIVISION FOR EARLY CHILDHOOD
OF THE COUNCIL FOR EXCEPTIONAL CHILDREN**

Eva M. Horn and Hazel Jones
Co-Editors

Disclaimer

The opinions and information contained in the articles in this publication are those of the authors of the respective articles and not necessarily those of the co-editors of the *Young Exceptional Children (YEC)* Monograph Series or of the Division for Early Childhood. Accordingly, the Division for Early Childhood assumes no liability or risk that may be incurred as a consequence, directly or indirectly, of the use and application of any of the contents of this publication.

The DEC does not perform due diligence on advertisers, exhibitors, or their products or services, and cannot endorse or guarantee that their offerings are suitable or accurate.

Copyright 2005 by the Division for Early Childhood of the Council for Exceptional Children. All rights reserved. 10 09   6 5 4 3 2

No portion of this book may be reproduced by any means, electronic or otherwise, without the express written permission of the Division for Early Childhood.

ISSN 1096-2506 • ISBN 978-0-9819327-3-6

Printed in the United States of America

Published and Distributed by:

Division for Early Childhood (DEC)
27 Fort Missoula Road, Suite 2
Missoula, MT 59804
(406) 543-0872 • FAX (406) 543-0887
www.dec-sped.org

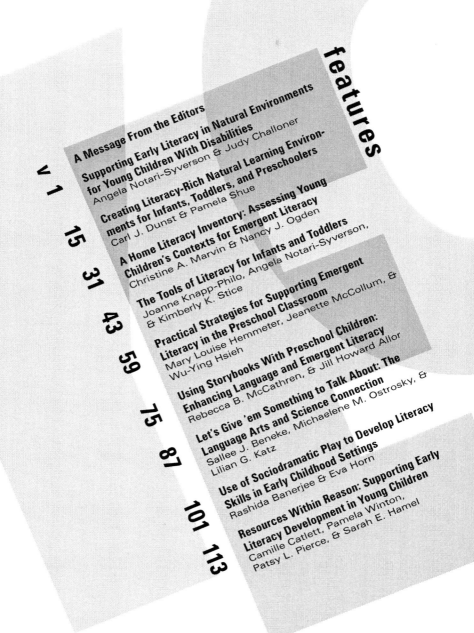

A Message From the Editors

Welcome to the seventh issue of the *Young Exceptional Children* (*YEC*) Monograph Series. The topic for this issue is the support of early literacy development in young children. A monograph focusing on early literacy is certainly timely given the national attention directed to both the achievement of reading competency by America's school children and on early educational opportunities to promote children's school success. In accordance with the joint position of the International Reading Association (IRA) and the National Association for the Education of Young Children (NAEYC) (http://www.naeyc. org/about/positions/psread0.asp), literacy development or reading and writing acquisition is viewed as a developmental continuum rather than an all-or-nothing phenomenon. Furthermore, although reading and writing abilities continue to develop throughout the life span, the early childhood years—from birth through age eight—are the most important period for literacy development. But the ability to read and write does not develop naturally, without careful planning and instruction.

The recognition of the critical role of careful planning and effective instruction in supporting the growth and development of young children with disabilities and other special needs is a foundational component of DEC's Recommended Practices in early intervention/early childhood special education (Sandall, Hemmeter, Smith, & McLean, 2004). One of our goals with each *YEC* monograph is to link the articles with key aspects of DEC's Recommended Practices. Each of the authors of the eight articles in this monograph discusses the importance of planning; of establishing literacy-rich, engaging environments; and of careful attention to adults' roles in supporting young children's discovery and learning. The authors also write about embedding or incorporating careful instruction within ongoing routines and activities of the home, community, or classroom. It is within this frame that the articles in this monograph provide guidance to early educators, family members, and caregivers as they seek to support the development of literacy in young children in their care.

Another goal of the *YEC* Monograph Series is to translate research findings into effective and useful strategies for practitioners and families. Thus, the articles provide readers with information and resources for further study to understand the theory or research upon which the practices described are based. Yet, each author has prepared a reader-friendly article written for a broad audience. Technical terms are explained and information is frequently augmented with descriptions, vignettes, or examples to enhance the reader's understanding.

The first three articles begin the discussion of early literacy by focusing on the environment and how the adults in young children's lives can enhance the environment to support young children's learning. The first article, by Notari-Syverson and Challoner, offers suggestions for early interventionists and early childhood special educators on how to support families in enhancing their young children's literacy development. They describe effective strategies to encourage family involvement in the early literacy development of young children with disabilities in home and community environments. Dunst and Shue follow with information on the importance of using everyday natural learning activities as contexts for promoting the development of infants, toddlers, and preschoolers. Through the presentation of a simple but useful model, they illustrate the relationship between everyday literacy activities and later literacy development. They close their article with specific examples of the kinds of everyday activities that research indicates are important experiences for promoting early literacy development. The final of the three articles focusing on the environmental context for literacy development is by Marvin and Odgen. In their article, they provide a tool for assessing and understanding the literacy environments in which young children live, the "Home Literacy Inventory." In addition, not only do they provide the tool and describe its use for collecting information, but they advise the reader on what to do with the information once it has been collected.

In the next two articles the focus shifts from the environment to specific activities and strategies for promoting language and literacy learning. Knapp-Philo, Notari-Syverson, and Stice describe a "Tools of Literacy" framework for infants and toddlers. The framework is designed to support adults, particularly within home or home care settings, to intentionally use a wide variety of developmentally appropriate literacy tools, thereby providing infants and toddlers with increased opportunities to build a broad foundation for their future literacy learning. While also providing the reader with specific activities, Hemmeter, McCollum, and Hsieh focus their attention on the preschool-age child and the preschool classroom. They describe the process of embedding literacy teaching strategies into the current curriculum of the early childhood classroom. Multiple practical strategies for addressing specific literacy outcomes across the routines and activities of the preschool day are described and then illustrated through vignettes.

The final three articles highlight the notion of embedding early literacy content within the natural routines and activities of young children's lives. McCathren and Allor begin with the very familiar and important context for all young children, storybook reading. They discuss specific strategies for using storybooks with preschoolers to facilitate language development and emergent literacy skills. They guide the reader through each element of the strategies of storybook preview, storybook read aloud, and storybook celebration. Beneke, Ostrosky, and Katz follow with a discussion of using science and discovery as the foundation for language and literacy learning. The purpose of their article is to provide teachers with information on how to prepare and organize the classroom environment for supporting children's exploration and discussion, and for connecting language and literacy with science. Specifically, guidelines for constructing an area that is rich in literacy and science content, and for introducing a new science theme, are described and illustrated through vignettes. Banerjee and Horn, in the final article, discuss the relationship between literacy and play, particularly sociodramatic play. They provide descriptions of the integration of early literacy and sociodramatic play with the role of the early educator, plus strategies to enhance the environment to facilitate sociodramatic play and incorporate literacy content.

This seventh monograph ends, as have the previous issues, with Catlett's "Resources Within Reason." As in each issue of *Young Exceptional Children (YEC)* magazine, Catlett and her colleagues identify for readers low cost but high quality resources, in this case those that support adults' efforts in providing early literacy experiences for young children.

As you read the articles in this monograph, we hope that they accomplish a number of objectives. First, we hope that as practitioners you are inspired to reflect upon your practices with young children and their families in addressing early literacy learning and that you are validated for what you are already doing. Second, we hope the articles shed new light on your practices or give you some new ideas. Third, we hope that they remind you that we, as a field, have evidence that we must use to guide our planning and interventions. We extend out sincere thanks to all the reviewers who contributed to this issue of the *Young Exceptional Children* Monograph series.

Contributing Reviewers
Wendy Arnold, Georgia College and State University, Milledgeville, GA
Rashida Banerjee, University of Kansas at Lawrence
Ann Bingham, University of Nevada-Reno
Patty Blasco, Portland State University, OR
Gretchen Butera, Indiana University at Bloomington
Virginia Buysse, University of North Carolina at Chapel Hill
Paige Campbell, Georgia College and State University, Milledgeville, GA
Lynette Chandler, Northern Illinois University, Dekalb, IL
Amy Childre, Georgia College and State University, Milledgeville, GA
Nitasha Clark, Vanderbilt University, Nashville, TN
Laurie Dinnebeil, University of Toledo, OH
Paddy Favazza, University of Memphis, TN
Lise Fox, University of South Florida

Misty Goosen, University of Kansas at Lawrence
Joan Grim, Vanderbilt University, Nashville, TN
Sarah Hadden, University of Virginia
Marci Hanson, San Francisco State University
Sanna Harjusola Webb, University of Kansas at Lawrence
Mary Louise Hemmeter, University of Illinois at Urbana-Champaign
Pamela Howard, University of Alabama, Tuscaloosa
Ronda Jenson, University of Missouri, Kansas City
Lee Ann Jung, University of Kentucky
Gwiok Kim, University of Kansas
Cecile Komara, University of Kansas
Angel Lee, University of Illinois at Urbana-Champaign
Joan Lieber, University of Maryland
David Lindeman, University of Kansas
Marisa Macy, University of Oregon
Chris Marvin, University of Nebraska
Katherine McCormick, University of Kentucky
Linda Mitchell, Wichita State University, KS
Chryso Mouzourou, University of Illinois at Urbana-Champaign
Chelie Nelson, University of Kansas
Melissa Olive, University of Texas at Austin
Susan Palmer, University of Kansas
Carla Peterson, Iowa State University
Ilka Pfister, University of Delaware
Diane Plunkett, University of Kansas at Lawrence
Kristi Pretti-Frontczak, Kent State University, OH
Paige Pullen, University of Virginia
Megan Purcell, Eastern Kentucky University, Richmond
Cathy Qi, West Chester University, Newark
Sharon Rosenkoetter, Oregon State University, Corvallis
Yumiko Saito, University of Kansas
Rosa Milagros Santos, University of Illinois at Urbana-Champaign
Ilene Schwartz, University of Washington at Seattle
Amanda Terrell, University of Kansas at Lawrence
Dawn Thomas, University of Illinois at Urbana-Champaign
Vickie Turbiville, Dripping Springs, TX
Dale Walker, University of Kansas at Lawrence
Robin Wells, Eastern New Mexico State University, Portales

Reference

Sandall, S., Hemmeter, M. L., Smith, B., & McLean, M. (Eds.). (2004). *DEC recommended practices: A comprehensive guide for practical application in early intervention/early childhood special education.* Longmont, CO: Sopris West.

Co-Editors: Eva Horn   Hazel Jones
                   evahorn@ku.edu   HAjones@coe.ufl.edu

Coming Next!

The topic for the eighth *YEC* Monograph is "Social-Emotional Development." For more information, check the "Announcements" section of *Young Exceptional Children* (Volume 9, Number 1) or visit **http:/www.dec-sped.org.**

Supporting Early Literacy in Natural Environments for Young Children With Disabilities

Angela Notari-Syverson, Ph.D., and Judy Challoner, M.Ed.,
Washington Research Institute, Seattle, WA

Five-year old David is at the Asian grocery store with his grandmother. He is very interested in the boxes of fruit candies on display for the Lunar New Year. Together they discuss which ones to buy. David's grandmother helps him recognize the contents from the pictures of fruit on the labels. She also points out how the words on the labels are written in both English and Vietnamese. David recognizes some letters of the English words. His grandmother reads the words in Vietnamese and David translates the words into English.

Four-year old Nadia is on the bus with her father, who just picked her up from child care. They look at billboards, road signs, and the signs and advertisements on the bus. They talk about what they see through the window. Nadia sees a seagull and joyfully exclaims: "Seagulls, bald eagles, they rhyme!" She repeats this phrase multiple times and even makes it into a song.

Three-year old Laura snuggles with her mother to look at the photographs her aunt sent from Mexico. They place the pictures in the family photo album and Laura's mother writes small captions describing the people and places in each photo. They talk about the pictures and Laura's mother tells Laura stories about Mexico and her childhood. She teaches Laura her favorite childhood song.

Everyday routines in the home, at child care, and in the neighborhood provide many opportunities for young children to engage in experiences with different aspects of literacy (Orellana & Hernandez, 1999). Well before they begin school, children acquire important knowledge about print and books; use of literate types of language; and awareness of sounds that prepare them for later, more formal learning about literacy in school (Burns, Griffin, & Snow, 1999; Heath, 1982). As children interact with caregivers around daily objects and activities—for example, sorting through the mail, recognizing a logo on a paper bag, talking about a graphic on a piece of clothing while getting dressed, tracing figures with a stick in the sand—they learn critical early social, cognitive, and language behaviors that are the foundation for later literacy (Notari-Syverson, in press). In the opening vignette we see that David, at the grocery store, learns how pictures and print provide important information. On the bus, Nadia learns conversational and narrative skills and develops sensitivity to words and sounds, while Laura, at home, learns about her mother's native culture through photographs, writing, and song.

As children interact with caregivers around daily objects and activities—for example, sorting through the mail, recognizing a logo on a paper bag, talking about a graphic on a piece of clothing while getting dressed, tracing figures with a stick in the sand—they learn critical early social, cognitive, and language behaviors that are the foundation for later literacy ....

The purpose of this article is to offer suggestions for early intervention and early childhood special educators on how to support families in enhancing their young children's literacy development. We describe some effective strategies to encourage family involvement in the early literacy development of young children with disabilities in home and community environments. But first, a brief summary of the rationale for including families of young children with disabilities in literacy development and a brief description of the basic components of early literacy are presented.

Rationale for Family Involvement in Literacy Development

Parental activities at home involving early language and literacy are strong predictors of children's school achievement (Dickinson & DeTemple, 1998; Sénéchal & LeFevre, 2002). Parents who talk with their children, look at picture books with them, read books for their own enjoyment, have a variety of books in the home, and go to the library are teaching their children that literacy is a valuable and meaningful family activity. Children who at an early age experience reading and writing as pleasurable and important are more successful later in school (Paratore, Melzi, & Krol-Sinclair, 1999). Children who come from homes where oral traditions, visual media (e.g., television, videos), and popular print are stressed, on the other hand, may not become as fluent in the more formal types of language and literacy used in the schools (e.g., reading books, writing, and using educational materials) (Makin & Diaz, 2002). Families who view literacy as just "books" or as "work" rather than an activity to engage in for personal enjoyment and pleasure may be unaware of the multiple ways literacy is part of daily life.

While literacy activities are an integral part of daily environments and all children can participate in literacy activities at some level, many professionals and families still think of literacy activities as inappropriate for young children with disabilities (McNaught, 2002; Notari-Syverson, 2004). Children with disabilities tend to have less exposure to print and fewer opportunities to interact with adults in literacy-related activities (Marvin & Mirenda, 1993). Often, home literacy activities for preschool children with disabilities are limited to only a few activities, such as storybook reading (Fitzgerald, Roberts, Schuele, & Coleman, 1991). Also, mothers of children with special needs tend to use language consisting of directives and test questions rather than comments and questions encouraging more elaborated responses that in turn develop oral language skills (Hart & Risley, 1995)

Providing families with resources and supports to strengthen family participation and acquisition of new knowledge and skills is an important component of early intervention and early childhood special education services (Sandall, Hemmeter, Smith, & McLean, 2005). Family literacy resources currently available, however, provide little information on specific kinds of instructional supports and strategies for families to use with their young children who have disabilities. Also, many of these resources require good reading ability and may, therefore, not be accessible to all families who are not well versed in formal types of literacy.

Components of a Comprehensive Approach to Early Literacy

Preparing preschool children to become good readers and writers involves supporting multiple skills including print awareness, phonological awareness, and oral language (Burns et al., 1999; Lonigan, Burgess, Anthony, & Barker, 1998; Notari-Syverson, O'Connor, & Vadasy, 1998). These skills are interrelated and mutually influence each other throughout the developmental period (Dickinson, McCabe, Anastasopoulos, Peisner-Feinberg, & Poe, 2003; Storch & Whitehurst, 2002). We examine each in turn to better illuminate the concept and highlight some opportunities that adults have to teach these skills to young children during daily activities.

Print awareness involves facilitating the development and use of a variety of graphic and written symbols (e.g., objects, gestures, pictures, drawing, signs, letters, numbers, maps) as tools for communicating ideas and acquiring knowledge. In the vignette, David, at the grocery store, uses pictures on labels to recognize the product. His interest extends to the letters and words in two different scripts on the labels, presenting an excellent opportunity for an adult to teach him letter names and sounds. Similarly, Nadia, on the bus, learns to recognize road signs, and words and letters on billboards and advertisements on the bus. Laura learns how pictures and writing represent real people and places, and how writing is connected to what one says.

Phonological awareness involves encouraging children to play with words and sounds and to build awareness that spoken words not only have meaning but also have specific sound characteristics that affect their meaning (e.g., changing "dog" to "log"). Nadia finds similarities between the sounds of words ("seagulls" and "eagles") and takes pleasure in repeating verses. For David, learning English and Vietnamese will help him become more aware of the different sound characteristics of words. Laura learns a new song with rhyming words in Spanish.

Oral language involves developing vocabulary, syntax, narratives, and the use of more formal literate types of oral language for talking about abstract ideas, events that happened in the past, predicting what will happen in the future, imagining fictional situations and stories, and using language for critical thinking and scientific purposes. These literate discourse skills are critical for later reading and writing tasks asked of children in elementary school and beyond. David asks questions about foods he is interested in and his grandmother explains the contents. Nadia and her father talk about different things they see from the bus. Laura listens to her mother talk about growing up in a different culture. Together they converse about different foods, games, songs, and childhood activities.

Model for Supporting Family Participation in Early Literacy Development

Successful approaches to family involvement must take into account multiple aspects related to both child development and adult learning. These aspects include, but are not limited to, the family's daily environments, the characteristics of the child, interactions between the child and caregiver, and the caregiver's interest and motivation in literacy activities. We know that young children learn best about literacy through meaningful everyday life activities that integrate different language, cognitive, and social-emotional developmental skills (Burns et al., 1999).

Furthermore, all children, including those with disabilities, develop and learn primarily from engaging in social interactions, referred to as scaffolding, during which an adult guides and supports the child's learning by building on what the child is able to do (Berk & Winsler, 1995). During daily activities, caregivers scaffold with children in numerous ways: modeling, encouraging, providing meaning to activities, giving directions for tasks, or adapting materials so that they are appropriate for the child's interest and developmental level. For example, when David has trouble recognizing the winter melon from the picture on the label, his grandmother takes him to the produce aisle and shows him the real fruit. They check the label and then weigh the fruit. Nadia's father builds on her enjoyment of rhyming by making the interaction more challenging for her. He introduces her to an "I Spy" game involving things that start with the same first sound (e.g., seagull, sand, sea). Laura has difficulty turning the thin pages of the photo album so her mother adds some clothes pegs to the pages to make them easier to manipulate. She also finds a photo of Laura and writes Laura's name in big letters on a strip of paper to help Laura better understand the connection between the picture and the spoken and written word. They converse back and forth in English and Spanish about family members and their photographs.

During daily activities, caregivers scaffold with children in numerous ways: modeling, encouraging, providing meaning to activities, giving directions for tasks, or adapting materials so that they are appropriate for the child's interest and developmental level.

Finally, from adult learning theory, we know that participatory learning or learning that focuses on issues and needs that are important to the learners themselves is more effective for adults, including family members (Freire & Macedo, 1987). This implies that home literacy activities must also be meaningful for the family. Making a grocery list, sorting the mail, and looking up a telephone number are common family activities involving literacy.

Keys to Family Involvement

A key component of any model designed to provide support and information to families is that it allows for multiple and flexible ways for families to access and engage the content (Trivette & Dunst, 2005). Verbal presentations, print materials, modeling, coaching, and videotapes have been used to communicate with and to provide information to families and caregivers. Different formats may be better suited to different groups. For example, families who have high English literacy skills may favor written materials, while families with low literacy skills in English may prefer alternative formats such as direct communication, picture books, audiotapes, and videotapes (Kalyanpur & Harry, 1999; Turnbull & Ruef, 1996). A combination of formats that allows families choices is probably the most effective with families across the range of skills and preferences that early intervention providers encounter.

> *A key component of any model designed to provide support and information to families is that it allows for multiple and flexible ways for families to access and engage the content ....*

The following suggestions for both strategies and materials were developed specifically for children with disabilities and field tested by families and ECSE professionals in the context of a model demonstration project funded by the Office of Special Education Programs (Notari-Syverson, 2002). These strategies and materials incorporate the philosophical foundations that we have identified as critical to a quality family involvement program for early literacy development, which are: (1) provides activities that address a continuum of early literacy skills; (2) ensures that all activities are ones that families can easily integrate into their daily routines; (3) includes strategies for families to support their child's specific learning needs; and (4) builds upon the assumption that families view helping their children's literacy learning as important and rewarding for both their children and themselves. Six different strategies and materials are described in the following sections: literacy activities involving print materials; strategies for sharing informational materials; literacy bags for supporting the family's home literacy activities; strategies for modeling use of home literacy activities; portfolios as tools for connecting home and school literacy activities; and videotapes as tools for teaching families language facilitation strategies.

Literacy Activities Involving Print Materials

It is critical that print materials are jargon free, use simple language, and contain concrete examples and illustrations. Materials can include suggestions of activities (e.g., in class newsletters) or materials that teachers can send home for caregivers and children to complete together and then send back to school (e.g., blank children's journals; books with simple "review" forms; a booklet for caregivers to fill in with pictures and dictations from their child).

The "Literacy Activities for Caregivers and Young Children (LACYC)" (Notari-Syverson et al., 2004) were developed based upon the *Ladders to Literacy* activities for children and parents (Notari-Syverson et al., 1998), a set of written suggestions of practical everyday early literacy activities for families to use at home. Each LACYC activity has simple suggestions for adults of ways to engage in literacy activities with children during daily routines, and also includes two levels of scaffolding suggestions or "Hints" (i.e., "To help your child succeed … " and "To make this activity more challenging … "). Figure 1 shows an example of an LACYC literacy activity.

Figure 1
Example of a Literacy Activity for Caregivers and Young Children (LACYC): Seeing First Words

Activity

Seeing first words

- Your child will recognize words on food packaging, buildings, and other things.
- See if your child can see any other words.
- Ask your child questions about these words ("What do we do with Cheerios?").

Hints

Seeing first words

To help your child succeed, you can:
- Point to words your child often sees (McDonald's or Cheerios) and ask your child what the words are.
- Say words you see and point to them.
- Show an object or picture that corresponds to the word.
- Ask your child simple questions about words he or she sees ("Do we eat Cheerios?").

To make this activity more challenging, you can:
- Ask your child how he or she knows they are words.
- Ask your child where else he or she sees words.
- See if your child knows the difference between a picture, a word, and a number.
- Ask your child questions to make him or her really think ("What else could we do with Cheerios?").

Note: Reprinted with permission from Notari-Syverson et al., 2004.

Strategies for Sharing Informational Materials

Other print materials can focus on providing information to parents on language and literacy development, different purposes and functions of literacy, and how the home activities help better prepare children to be successful later in school. These materials can consist of short and simple handouts, and booklets or brochures specifically designed for families with low literacy skills. Topics can include phonological awareness, book conventions, and emergent writing skills. Teachers can use them with parents during home visits, at Individualized Education Plan or Individualized Family Services Plan (IEP/IFSP) meetings, or during parent nights and/or other family involvement events.

Literacy Bags for Supporting the Family's Home Literacy Activities

Print materials alone may not provide sufficient guidance for caregivers about what to do to enhance literacy. Also, many families lack necessary literacy materials at home. Sending home "literacy bags" provides caregivers with clear, concrete examples of materials and activities. The preparation of the bags and the development of a system to manage their use will require an initial time investment. Literacy bags can be designed to focus on specific print awareness, phonological sensitivity, and oral language skills. Each bag will include a clear description of activities (much like the LACYC activities described previously), materials relevant to the activities, and a simple form for parents to provide feedback to teachers on how they used the literacy bag. Table 1 shows examples of themes, activities, and materials for 12 different literacy bags, adapted from literacy bags originally developed by the Auburn School District Early Childhood Team, Auburn, WA.

Strategies for Modeling Use of Home Literacy Activities

Home visits provide an effective tool for professionals to model and provide feedback on the use of literacy bags or other language and literacy activities using objects from the home during a family's daily routines (Saint Laurent, Giasson, & Couture, 1998). Teachers can also invite parents to the classroom, model literacy activities, and have parents practice with their child.

Table 1
Literacy Bag Ideas

Theme	Activities	Materials	Language & Literacy Skills
Names, Letters, Signs	• Making a book • Reading a book • Taking dictations • Drawing and writing	Magnetic letters Crayons Shaving cream Alphabet stamps and inkpads Paper Sticky notes Note cards Alphabet book (e.g., *Chicka Chicka Boom Boom* by P. Martin)	• Knowledge of letter names and sounds • Recognizing environmental print • Recognizing own name in print • Understanding the connection between oral and written language
Conversations	• Talking about food • TV shows • What happened in the past, what will happen next • Making a book	Book about food Books about actions Paper Crayons	• Turn taking • Vocabulary • Narrative • Understanding the connection between oral and written language
Sound and Word Games	• Playing sound and word/phonics games	Alphabet cards ABC match games	• Knowledge of letter names and sounds • Identifying first sounds in words • Blending and segmenting syllables
Making Up Stories	• Looking at picture books • Making a diary • Drawing and writing • Taking dictations	Crayons Markers Paper Stickers Tools for making a book (ribbon, hole punch, safety scissors) Picture book (e.g., *Cookie's Week* by C. Ward & T. dePaola)	• Vocabulary • Narrative • Understanding the connection between oral and written language
Learning About Rhymes	• Looking at picture books • Playing rhyming games • Talking about the sounds in words	Magnetic letters Rhyme matching games Book with rhyming words (e.g., *Jamberry* by B. Degen)	• Listening • Playing with sounds • Rhyming

Table 1 (*continued*)

Theme	Activities	Materials	Language & Literacy Skills
Playing With Sounds and Rhyming Words	• Talking about nursery rhymes • Coloring pictures of nursery rhymes • Talking about words and sounds	Book of nursery rhymes Nursery rhyme coloring sheets Crayons	• Listening • Playing with sounds and words • Talking about patterns in rhyming words • Learning nursery rhymes
Looking at Books/ Prereading	• Looking at picture books • Getting a library card	Picture book Page fluffers and aids for turning pages (e.g., clothes pegs) Library card application form	• Learning about book and print conventions • Talking about pictures in books • Talking about a story
Measuring Things	• Measuring things • Writing	Small notebook Tape measure String Unifix cubes Measuring cups and spoons Number tiles Picture book about measuring	• Learning that literacy is more than reading and writing • Learning about different functions and purposes of print
Going Places	• Talking about things outside • Going to the grocery store, library, and park • Looking at picture books	Photographs or pictures of different places Picture books about different places (e.g., library, zoo) Containers (paper bags, egg cartons, used plastic containers) for "treasures" found outside	• Vocabulary • Recognizing environmental print • Learning about different purposes and functions of print
Making Maps	• Talking about the neighborhood • Making maps	Crayons Markers Paper Mapquest map of child's school location Book about maps	• Learning about different forms of written communication • Learning about different functions and purposes of print

Table 1 (*continued*)

Theme	Activities	Materials	Language & Literacy Skills
Music and Songs	• Listening to music • Singing • Making/playing a musical instrument	Book of songs Music CD Music makers Paper plates Rubber bands	• Listening • Vocabulary
Making Books	• Making a touch book or picture book	Paper Stapler Safety scissors Glue stick Bubblewrap, mylar, sponge, cotton balls, brillo pad, yarn Thick cover for book Sample board book	• Learning about book conventions • Learning about different types of books • Vocabulary • Narrative

Note: Adapted with permission from literacy bags developed by the Auburn School District Early Childhood Team, Auburn, WA.

Portfolios as Tools for Connecting Home and School Literacy Activities

Portfolios can be used successfully with both typically developing children and children with disabilities (Lynch & Struewing, 2001; Meisels, 1993). Inviting parents to contribute to their child's portfolio is an effective and meaningful way to enhance parent-teacher interactions and increase parents' awareness of their role in their child's learning (Losardo & Notari-Syverson, 2001). Teachers can send home samples of children's work and photographs of children engaged in classroom literacy activities. Families can share information with teachers by sending samples of children's drawings, titles of books read, lists of favorite songs and rhymes, anecdotes, and photographs documenting other literacy-related behaviors. Such participation (e.g., home literacy portfolios and a family-friendly checklist) helps parents be more actively involved in developing early literacy goals for their child's IEP/IFSP and assessing their child's progress.

Videotapes as Tools for Teaching Families Language Facilitation Strategies

Videotapes are an effective tool for supporting families in implementing learning strategies for language facilitation (e.g., Dale et al., 1996;

Lim & Cole, 2002; Whitehurst et al., 1988). Videotapes can be shown to parents during a parent night or lent out for parents to view at home. The *Language Is the Key* videotapes for families of young children with disabilities (Cole & Maddox, 1997) shows high-quality examples of strategies demonstrated by parents with their own children in natural settings to facilitate language and emergent literacy skills. The videotapes are available in English, Spanish, and other languages.

Conclusion

Literacy practices differ according to culture and context and may include oral stories, songs, music, dances, paintings, as well as the popular culture of television shows, cartoons, video games, computer icons, and movies (Makin & Diaz, 2002). It is important that literacy activities address practices that are meaningful for families, especially for families from cultures that emphasize storytelling and other oral forms of literacy over print. Also professionals need to be aware of linguistic differences in sounds and rhymes and the need to encourage families to use their primary language in activities related to oral language, sound play, and phonological sensitivity. When suggesting specific activities professionals should also consider possible cultural differences related to gender issues (e.g., cooking) and religion (e.g., role of music), and the need to make sure activities and routines are meaningful and accessible for all families (e.g., going to the store and the park, rather than the zoo or museums). Above all, it is important to validate what families are already doing, and to make sure families feel successful no matter what they do. Information and materials should address the issue of balancing respect for individual cultures with preparing all children to meet the cultural expectations of the mainstream school environment.

Above all, it is important to validate what families are already doing, and to make sure families feel successful no matter what they do. Information and materials should address the issue of balancing respect for individual cultures with preparing all children to meet the cultural expectations of the mainstream school environment.

Note
You can reach Angela Notari-Syverson by e-mail at anotari@wri-edu.org

References
Berk, L., & Winsler, A. (1995). *Scaffolding children's learning: Vygotsky and early childhood education*. Washington, DC: National Association for the Education of Young Children (NAEYC).

Burns, S., Griffin, P., & Snow, C. (Eds.). (1999). *Starting out right: A guide to promoting children's reading success*. Washington, DC: National Academy Press.

Cole, K., & Maddox, M. (1997). *Language is the key* (Video). Seattle, WA: Washington Learning Systems (www.walearning.com).

Dale, P., Crain-Thoreson, C., Notari-Syverson, A., & Cole, K. (1996). Parent-child storybook reading as an intervention technique for young children with language delays. *Topics in Early Childhood Special Education, 16*, 213–235.

Dickinson, D., & DeTemple, J. (1998). Putting parents in the picture: Maternal reports of preschoolers' literacy as a predictor of early reading. *Early Childhood Research Quarterly, 13*, 241–261.

Dickinson, D., McCabe, A., Anastasopoulos, L., Peisner-Feinberg, E., & Poe, M. (2003). The comprehensive language approach to early literacy: The interrelationships among vocabulary, phonological sensitivity, and print knowledge among preschool-aged children. *Journal of Educational Psychology, 95*(3), 465–481.

Fitzgerald, J., Roberts, J., Schuele, M., & Coleman, P. (1991, December). *Emerging literacy development of preschool handicapped children*. Paper presented at the National Reading Conference, Palm Springs, CA.

Freire, P., & Macedo, D. (1987). *Literacy: Reading the word and reading the world*. Westport, CT: Bergin & Garvey.

Hart, B., & Risley, T. (1995). *Meaningful differences in the everyday experience of young American children*. Baltimore: Paul H. Brookes.

Heath, S. B. (1982). What no bedtime story means: Narrative skills at home and at school. *Language in Society, 11*, 49–78.

Kalyanpur, M., & Harry, B. (1999). *Culture in special education: Building reciprocal family-professional relationships*. Baltimore: Paul H. Brookes.

Lim, Y. S., & Cole, K. (2002). Facilitating first language development in young Korean children through parent training in picture book interactions. *Bilingual Research Journal, 26*(2), 213–227.

Lonigan, C., Burgess, S., Anthony, J., & Barker, T. (1998). Development of phonological sensitivity in 2- to 5-year old children. *Journal of Educational Psychology, 90*(2), 294–311.

Losardo, A., & Notari-Syverson, A. (2001). *Alternative approaches to assessing young children*. Baltimore: Paul H. Brookes.

Lynch, E. M., & Struewing, N. A. (2001). Children in context: Portfolio assessment in the inclusive early childhood classroom. *Young Exceptional Children, 5*(1), 2–10.

Makin, L., & Diaz, C. J. (2002). *Literacies in early childhood: Changing views, challenging practices*. Baltimore: Paul H. Brookes.

Marvin, C., & Mirenda, P. (1993). Home literacy experiences of preschoolers enrolled in Head Start and special education programs. *Journal of Early Intervention, 17*, 351–367.

McNaught, M. (2002). Literacy for all? Young children and special literacy learning needs. In L. Makin & C. J. Diaz (Eds.), *Literacies in early childhood: Changing views, challenging practices* (pp. 233–249). Baltimore: Paul H. Brookes.

Meisels, S. (1993). Remaking classroom assessment with the work sampling system. *Young Children*, 34–40.

Notari-Syverson, A. (in press). Everyday tools of literacy. In S. Rosenkoetter & J. Knapp-Philo (Eds.), *Learning to read the world: Language and literacy in the first three years*. Washington, DC: Zero to Three Press.

Notari-Syverson, A. (2004). Literacy for all children: Scaffolding early language and literacy in young children with special needs. *Children and Families, 28*(1), 48–52.

Notari-Syverson, A. (2002). *Scaffolding emergent literacy: Supporting the early literacy development of young children with disabilities in natural environments* (OSEP Model Demonstration Funded Grant # H324M020084). Seattle, WA: Washington Research Institute.

Notari-Syverson, A., O'Connor, R., & Vadasy, P. (1998). *Ladders to literacy: A preschool activity book*. Baltimore: Paul H. Brookes.

Notari-Syverson, A., Rytter, K., Challoner, J., Sadler, F., Lim, Y., Sturm, M., & Hedlund, R. (2004). *Literacy activities for caregivers and young children* (Unpublished manual). Seattle, WA: Washington Research Institute.

Orellana, M., & Hernandez, A. (1999). Talking the walk: Children reading urban environmental print. *The Reading Teacher, 52*(6), 612–619.

Paratore, J., Melzi, G., & Krol-Sinclair, B. (1999). *What can we expect of family literacy? Experiences of Latino children whose parents participated in an intergenerational literacy project*. Newark, DE: International Reading Association.

Saint-Laurent, L., Giasson, J., & Couture, C. (1998). Emergent literacy and intellectual disabilities. *Journal of Early Intervention, 21*, 267–281.

Sandall, S., Hemmeter, M. L., Smith, B., & McLean, M. (Eds.). (2005). *DEC recommended practices in early intervention/early childhood special education: A comprehensive guide for practical application*. Longmont, CO: Sopris West.

Sénéchal, M., & LeFevre, J. (2002). Parental involvement in the development of children's reading skill: A five-year longitudinal study. *Child Development, 73*, 445–460.

Storch, S. A., & Whitehurst, G. J. (2002). Oral language and code-related precursors to reading: Evidence from a longitudinal structural model. *Developmental Psychology, 38*, 934–947.

Trivette, C., & Dunst, C. (2005). Family-based practices. In S. Sandall, M. L. Hemmeter, B. J. Smith, & M. E. McLean (Eds.), *DEC recommended practices in early intervention/early childhood special education: A comprehensive guide for practical application* (pp. 107–126). Longmont, CO: Sopris West.

Turnbull, A., & Ruef, M. (1996). Family perspectives on family behavior. *Mental Retardation, 34*, 280–293.

Whitehurst, G. H., Falco, F. L., Lonigan, C. J., Fischel, J. E., Debaryshe, B. D., Valdez-Menchaca, M. C., & Caulfield, M. (1988). Accelerating language development through picture book reading. *Developmental Psychology, 24*, 552–559.

Creating Literacy-Rich Natural Learning Environments for Infants, Toddlers, and Preschoolers

Carl J. Dunst, Ph.D.,
Orelena Hawks Puckett Institute, Asheville, NC

Pamela Shue, Ed.M.,
J. Iverson Riddle Developmental Center, Morganton, NC

Veronica loves to draw circles, lines, and other shapes on the sidewalk outside her house using different colors of chalk. She has become especially proficient at drawing simple but clearly differentiated figures.

Sammy's ability to "print" his name using magnetic letters is uncanny. He is able to find all the letters in his name on an alphabet board, and spell it correctly almost every time.

A father takes his daughter, Mary, on regular outings to the community fish and duck pond. Feeding the fish and ducks, and the occasional birds who are looking for a "free meal," gets Mary to talk about the happenings and to ask questions about the "goings on."

Tasha and her mother delight in playing finger games and repeating rhymes while having fun time together. Tasha's ability to produce a rich variety of sounds and sound combinations is amazing to hear.

William just can't wait to have his mother read him his favorite book. If he had his way, his mother would have to read and reread the same story 100 times per day! William has so mastered the story line that he recognizes and talks about the upcoming events in the story just by seeing the pictures on the different pages of the book.

These are but a few examples of how everyday activities provide young children opportunities to learn and practice early literacy development skills. Cairney (2002) noted, based on available research, that the experiences children have day-in and day-out in their homes and in the community contribute to later literacy success in school.

This article is based on the authors' research and practice using everyday natural learning activities as contexts for promoting the development of infants, toddlers, and preschoolers. The article is divided into four sections. The first section includes descriptions of six literacy domains that constitute the focus of our research and practice. The second section presents a simple but useful model for showing the relationship between everyday literacy activities and later literacy development. The third section includes examples of the kinds of everyday activities that research indicates are important experiences for promoting early literacy development. The last section provides additional useful information for supporting children's literacy. The contents of this article provide information to be used to develop and implement interventions that support young children's literacy learning as part of their participation in everyday environments.

Preliteracy Domains of Development

Research on the literacy development of young children indicates that there are six domains of early literacy development: alphabetic awareness, print awareness, written language, comprehension (text and oral), phonological awareness, and oral language (Shue, 2005). Table 1 shows the definition of each literacy domain, which provide the foundation for understanding the particular kind of skills that are important indicators of early literacy development. The development of competencies in each domain constitutes the outcomes of the natural learning environment intervention practices described later in this article.

> *... [T]here are six domains of early literacy development: alphabetic awareness, print awareness, written language, comprehension (text and oral), phonological awareness, and oral language ....*

Alphabetic Awareness

Alphabetic awareness refers to a child's ability to recognize and name the letters of the alphabet in isolation, in the context of word recognition, and as part of word use (Whitehurst & Lonigan, 2001). Young children develop alphabetic awareness through opportunities to experiment with and write the alphabet (Armbruster, Lehr, & Osborn, 2003). Furthermore, engagement in activities such as singing alphabet songs, looking at alphabet books, and recognizing that letter combinations

Table 1

Six Domains of Preliteracy Development

Domain	Definition
Alphabetic Awareness	Ability to recognize the letters of the alphabet in the context of word recognition and word use. This includes the " ... translation of units of print (graphemes) to units of sound (phonemes) .... At the most basic level this requires the ability to distinguish letters" (Whitehurst & Lonigan, 2001, p. 14).
Print Awareness	Ability to recognize and "read" words and text accurately and quickly (fluency). This includes an understanding that books are read from front to back; how print appears and is placed on a page; and understanding that print carries meaning.
Written Language	Ability to represent ideas or words in a printed or written format. This includes learning to differentiate the elements of the written system (e.g., letters and words).
Comprehension	Ability to understand and process the meaning of ideas represented orally and in text. Reading comprehension is the process of simultaneously extracting and constructing meaning through interaction and involvement with written language consisting of three elements: text, reader, and activity/purpose for reading.
Phonological Awareness	Ability to recognize, manipulate, and use sounds in words, including the ability to hear and discriminate the sounds in language. Includes the " ... general ability to attend to the sounds of language as distinct from its meaning. Noticing similarities between words in their sounds, enjoying rhymes, counting syllables, and so forth are indicators of such metaphonological skills" (Snow, Burns, & Griffin, 1998, p. 52).
Oral Language	Ability to use words to communicate ideas and thoughts and to use language as a tool for deeper understanding. Oral language " ... consists of the use of words and rules for organizing words and changing them and the abilities to listen and accurately reconstruct what is said on the basis of understanding" (Roskos, Tabors, & Lenhart, 2004, pp. 6–7).

spell their own as well as other people's names are key contributors to the child's development of alphabetic awareness.

Print Awareness

Print awareness refers to a child's recognition of the characteristics and rules of written language (Strickland & Schickedanz, 2004). Print awareness includes the child's ability to understand that words in print have corresponding speech features, and that directionality is an important feature of printed text (e.g., reading left to right, top to bottom). Young children exposed to print in different forms across a variety of contexts and environments are more likely to develop the ability to recognize, point out, and read signs, labels, letters, words, etc., and ascribe meaning to printed materials.

Written Language

Written language refers to a child's ability to represent ideas and words in print (Dyson, 2002). When children learn to write the letters of the alphabet, print their name, and write other words, they develop an understanding of the conventions of print and written language. The markers of prewriting skills include, but are not limited to, scribbling, drawing, tracing, outlining, doodling, copying, and keyboarding. These kinds of skills provide young children the opportunity to represent thoughts, words, ideas, etc., in graphic formats.

Comprehension

Text and oral comprehension refers to a child's ability to read, listen, and process the meaning of ideas represented in text and spoken words (Snow, 2002). Comprehension is developed in the context of a child's working vocabulary, the ability to relate experiences to printed text, the ability to monitor one's understanding of printed material, and in oral transactions with others. Young children's experiences with materials, people, and experiences in the world provide them opportunities to acquire a larger vocabulary, which in turn provides the foundation for comprehension of the meaning of words in both written and oral formats.

Phonological Awareness

Phonological awareness refers to a child's ability to hear, identify, manipulate, and use sounds spoken in words (Snow, Burns, & Griffin, 1998). This includes, but is not limited to, rhyming, blending, and segmenting of sounds and words (Armbruster et al., 2003). The ability to recognize the similarities and differences in sounds is facilitated and enhanced by experiences that shape children's insights about sounds and sound segments in isolation and in combination.

Oral Language

Oral language refers to a child's ability to relate sounds to meaning that involve phonological (the rules for combining sounds), semantic (word meaning), and syntactic (rules that have to do with the order of words in sentences) components and elements of language use (Roskos, Tabors, & Lenhart, 2004). Oral language also includes a child's ability to use words to communicate ideas and thoughts through vocabulary, expressive language, and listening comprehension. The development of oral language is heavily dependent upon a "reason to talk," which is often influenced by the "interestingness" of objects, people, events, etc., in young children's environments (Nelson, 1999).

Preliteracy Development Model

Figure 1 shows a model that can guide efforts to engage children in everyday literacy learning environments and activities that promote the development of early literacy skills in each literacy domain (See Table 1). The development of early literacy skills in turn contributes to later literacy competence. The ultimate success of early literacy interventions is the development of later literacy competencies and abilities (i.e.,

Figure 1

Model Showing How Everyday Activities Provide Contexts for Preliteracy and Literacy Development

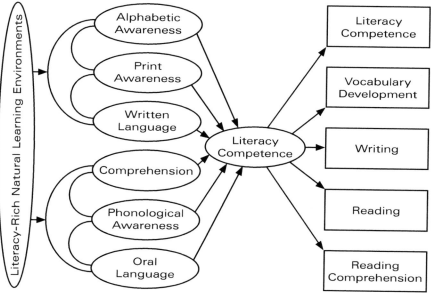

reading, writing, comprehension, etc.) (National Institute of Child Health and Human Development, 2000).

The ultimate success of early literacy interventions is the development of later literacy competencies and abilities ....

As described in the next section of this article, everyday literacy-rich natural environments are considered one source of experiences that shape and influence infants', toddlers', and preschoolers' emerging literacy skills. Our research (e.g., Bruder, Trivette, Dunst, & Hamby, 2000) as well as the research of others (see Neuman & Dickinson, 2002) highlights the importance of young children's participation in early literacy development activities. Figure 2, for example, shows findings from a study showing children's emerging participation in three typically occurring everyday literacy activities (Dunst, Hamby, Trivette, Raab, & Bruder, 2002). As can be seen in the figure, looking at books and reading or telling children stories become predominant activities by young children's first birthdays, and continue to be learning activities children experience throughout the preschool years.

The model shown in Figure 1 helps focus on the difference between the experiences and opportunities that are contexts for early literacy development and the consequences or skills that are developed by children as part of participation in the activities. We find it helpful to

Figure 2
Patterns of Preschoolers' Emerging Participation in Selected Everyday Literacy Activities

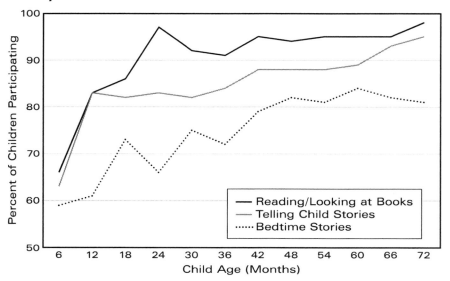

think of early literacy development as encompassing two broad sets of skills: (1) those involving *printed materials* (i.e., alphabetic awareness, print awareness, and written language); and (2) those involving *linguistic processing* (i.e., comprehension, phonological awareness, and oral language). Skill development in each set of skills as well as skill development in each specific literacy domain are viewed as the consequence of the experiences young children have as part of everyday living.

We also find it helpful to make a distinction between the types of everyday experiences children have as part of family and community life, and how different experiences are likely to have different behavioral and developmental consequences. For example, whereas finger games, rhyming games, and syllable clapping games are likely to be contexts for developing phonological awareness (Anthony & Lonigan, 2004), activities that involve running, climbing, and jumping are more likely to be contexts for developing motor coordination and muscle strength. The aim of literacy-based interventions is the engagement of children in literacy-rich experiences. This is why it is important to understand which everyday activities are and are not likely candidates for providing literacy-rich learning opportunities.

... [I]t is important to understand which everyday activities are and are not likely candidates for providing literacy-rich learning opportunities.

The provision of literacy learning opportunities that influence the development of literacy skills is expected to provide children the foundations for later literacy success. We know, for example, that early print, oral, and phonological awareness experiences are important for later literacy competence, including, but not limited to, reading and writing (Pullen & Justice, 2003).

Everyday Preliteracy Natural Learning Environments

An extensive review of the preliteracy and early literacy development research and practice literature was used to identify the everyday activities that provide infants, toddlers, and preschoolers learning opportunities shaping the acquisition of literacy competence (Shue & Dunst, in press-a). Our review specifically focused on those activities that research has found is empirically related to early literacy skill development. The reader is referred to www.everydaylearning.info/products.php for a bibliography of this research (see also Shue & Dunst, in press-b; Shue & Dunst, in press-c).

The research literature we reviewed was used to develop examples of everyday activities that could be used to provide children opportunities to learn, practice, and master early literacy development skills. The list of activities was also used to develop the "Early Literacy Experiences Scale" (Dunst, Raab, & Shue, in press). Parents completing the Scale are asked to indicate how often their child participates in the different literacy activities listed on the instrument. The Scale is modeled after instruments we have used in national studies of preschoolers' everyday natural learning environments (Dunst et al., 2000; Dunst et al., 2002). Our research has shown that young children's active participation in these everyday activities is related to a number of child and parent benefits (e.g., Dunst, Bruder, Trivette, & Hamby, in press; Trivette, Dunst, & Hamby, 2004).

... [R]esearch has shown that young children's active participation in these everyday activities is related to a number of child and parent benefits ....

Examples of the kinds of activities that are included on the "Early Literacy Experiences Scale" are shown in Table 2. The activities are

Table 2
Sources of Everyday Literacy-Rich Natural Learning Environment Experiences

Everyday Literacy Activities	Literacy Development Domains[a]					
	AA	PR	WL	CM	PA	OL
Reading street signs/store signs		X	X			
Picking out a movie at a video store		X	X			
Writing/scribbling on a chalkboard		X	X			
Looking at picture books		X	X			
Playing picture/card games		X	X			
Typing on a computer/keyboarding	X	X	X			
Making/writing birthday cards	X	X	X			
Coloring with crayons/magic markers	X		X			
Playing with alphabet stamps/blocks/letter magnets	X		X			
Drawing with a computer	X		X			
Looking at favorite pictures in a family photo album		X				

Table 2 (*continued*)

Everyday Literacy Activities	Literacy Development Domains[a]					
	AA	PR	WL	CM	PA	OL
Keeping a scrapbook of favorite pictures		X				
Gluing pictures on paper/in a diary		X				
Cutting pictures from a newspaper or magazine		X				
Looking at maps		X				
Reading familiar signs		X	X			X
Looking at the newspaper/comics/catalogs		X	X			
Looking at a picture dictionary	X	X				
Drawing/painting pictures	X	X				
Watching Sesame Street/Blues Clues				X		
Listening to books on tape				X		
Watching movies/videos				X		
Listening to storytellers				X		
Reading/listening to bedtime stories				X	X	
Listening to music				X		
Recording a story on a tape recorder					X	X
Playing games like "Peek-a-Boo" or "So Big"					X	X
Playing finger games/clapping games (e.g., Thumbkin, Five Little Monkeys)					X	X
Playing rhyming games					X	X
Making up/singing songs					X	X
Repeating jingles/phases from TV					X	X
Playing with puppets/stuffed animals					X	X
Dictating a shopping list					X	X
Saying nursery rhymes					X	X
Having mealtime conversations						X
Talking on the telephone				X		X
Having pretend phone conversations						X

Table 2 (*continued*)

Everyday Literacy Activities	Literacy Development Domains[a]					
	AA	PR	WL	CM	PA	OL
Talking about a child's favorite toys/ things to do				X		X
Looking at/reading cereal boxes		X	X			X
Playing card or board games	X	X			X	X
Reading/looking at books/magazines/ newspapers			X		X	
Looking at/reading restaurant menus		X	X	X	X	
Reading recipes		X	X		X	X
Writing letters or stories	X	X	X	X		
Visiting the library		X		X		
Going food shopping		X		X		
Family car/bus rides		X				X
Sending e-mails to friends/relatives	X	X	X		X	
Writing recipes	X	X	X		X	
Writing a shopping list	X	X	X		X	
Dictating a letter or story to an adult			X	X		X
Listening to story time at the library/ bookstore				X	X	X
Going to puppet shows				X		X
Visiting a children's museum		X		X		
Taking neighborhood/nature trail walks				X		X

[a] AA = Alphabetic awareness, PR = Print awareness, WL = Written language, CM = Comprehension, PA = Phonological awareness, OL = Oral language

organized by the type of experiences that have a high probability of influencing the development of different types of early literacy skills. Cairney and Ruge's (1998) compilation of literacy practices and was especially helpful in developing the classification presented in Table 2.

The activities in Table 2 are organized into three categories: (1) those that are important contexts for *print-related* competencies (i.e., alphabetic awareness, print awareness, and written language); (2) those that are important contexts for *linguistic processing* skills (i.e., comprehension, phonological awareness, and oral language); and (3) those that provide contexts for developing both sets of skills (i.e., multiple between-set domains). An "X" in the table indicates the particular literacy skills that are most likely to be developed in each literacy domain.

Print-Related Competencies

Alphabetic Awareness

Many different kinds of activities provide opportunities for developing alphabetic awareness including, but not limited to, playing with alphabet blocks, foam letters, letter magnets, letter stamps, etc. Many young children now have opportunities to "keyboard" and see letters appear on a computer monitor. Scrapbooks that include a different letter on each page in which children paste pictures and words starting with the different letters is an activity that can promote alphabetic awareness.

Print Awareness

Children's development of print awareness is most likely to occur through experiences that facilitate an understanding of symbols represented by pictures, images, words, etc. These print-rich activities include, but are not limited to, looking at a family photo album, looking at/reading comic strips, noticing symbols and words on cereal boxes, and so forth. Recognizing and "reading" street signs, restaurant signs, supermarket signs, etc., provide additional opportunities to associate symbols and print. Older preschoolers are likely to benefit from looking at and reading picture dictionaries.

Written Language

Any number of everyday activities that happen either routinely (e.g., coloring with markers or crayons) or as planned interventions (e.g., child making a shopping list) provide opportunities to develop prewriting and early writing skills. Activities that encourage drawing, painting, copying, and tracing are likely to be especially effective for developing prewriting skills. Typing words on a computer provides opportunities to see the words in a written format. Dictating or writing recipes, shopping lists, and e-mails or letters to friends or family members are other activities that promote understanding of the written language.

Linguistic Processing Skills

Comprehension

Both text and oral comprehension are enhanced by everyday activities such as listening to bedtime stories, parents' showing children newspapers and magazines, and identifying pictures or words in a book. Listening to storytellers, attending library story hours, and watching Sesame Street or Blues Clues are all activities that are likely to influence oral comprehension. "Reading" restaurant menus, anticipating the next events while looking at/reading a book, and picking out a movie at the video store are other activities that can promote text comprehension.

Phonological Awareness

The kinds of everyday activities that provide young children opportunities to acquire phonological awareness are generally the same kinds of activities that children find fun and enjoyable. The earliest phonological awareness skills are generally developed in the context of parent/child vocal interchanges, and especially as part of parent/child lap games (e.g., Peek-a-Boo). Finger games (e.g., Thumbkin, Five Little Monkeys, Itsy-Bitsy Spider, etc.), rhyming games, making up songs, repeating jingles, and repeating or writing poems are a few examples of activities that can promote sound sensitivity and discrimination in the middle preschool years. More sophisticated games such as "finding something that sounds like" can strengthen children's sensitivity to the similarities and differences in sounds.

Oral Language

Having pretend phone conversations, talking about favorite toys and people, and singing or saying nursery rhymes are examples of activities that provide contexts for oral expression. Research indicates that children are more likely to talk about and develop oral language skills in the context of participation in child interest-based activities (Nelson, 1999).

Supporting Literacy Learning in Everyday Activities

Promoting children's participation in everyday early literacy development activities is but one element of effective natural learning environment practices. Research demonstrates that the ways in which parents and other caregivers respond to children's emerging literacy skills, and encourage and support early literacy skill production, play important roles in influencing later literacy development.

... [T]he ways in which parents and other caregivers respond to children's emerging literacy skills, and encourage and support early literacy skill production, play important roles in influencing later literacy development.

Figure 3 shows a framework illustrating how literacy-rich everyday learning opportunities and instructional practices parents and caregivers use to support literacy learning facilitates and enhances literacy development (see Table 1). The everyday literacy activities and the ways in which parents and other caregivers support literacy learning are seen as interrelated intervention practices that enhance literacy learning in the six domains of our intervention model.

There are a number of instructional practices that are especially suited for facilitating and encouraging early literacy development in the context of everyday learning activities in the home and community. These include responsive teaching (Kaiser et al., 1996), scaffolding (Ukrainetz, Cooney, Dyer, Kysar, & Harris, 2000), and implicit instruction (Neuman & Roskos, 1993). Each of these strategies is easily used to support young children's literacy learning.

Figure 3
Framework for Integrating Three Elements of Early Literacy Development Intervention

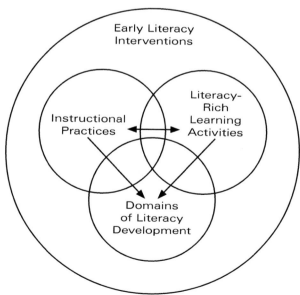

Responsive Teaching

Responsive or incidental teaching includes: (1) parent responsiveness (Trivette, 2003) to children's literacy behaviors as a way of maintaining child production of the behaviors; and (2) requests for elaborations (Seitz & Stewart, 1975) as a way of encouraging new or expanded literacy behaviors. A parent who shows excitement when his or her child recognizes a letter in the child's name (e.g.,"That's right! Your name does start with B.") and who asks the child to try to write or imitate the letters (e.g.,"Look! See what Bobby begins with.") is using a simple but powerful tool for encouraging literacy expression.

Scaffolding

Scaffolding is a particular type of elaboration strategy that includes the supports necessary for a child to demonstrate increased literacy competence (Rome-Flanders, Cronk, & Gourde, 1995). The strategy encourages active involvement of a child's production and mastery of literacy skills. The ultimate goal is the child's independent use of literacy skills as part of engagement in everyday activities involving print understanding and linguistic processing. A parent who is reading a book to a child and who provides "clues and hints" about the meaning of the printed text as a way of facilitating print awareness is using a simple scaffolding technique (e.g., "What do you think will happen next in the story?").

Implicit Instruction

Implicit instruction is a teaching strategy that focuses a child's attention on literacy expectations and provides him or her supports, guidance, and feedback in terms of the degree to which expectations were achieved (Neuman & Roskos, 1993). A parent who prompts a child to dictate a story in response to a child's experiences (e.g., "Tell me what happened when you saw the elephants at the zoo.") or who has a child make a shopping list in anticipation of an upcoming event (e.g., "What do we need to get when we go to the store?") is using the principles inherent in implicit instruction. Providing further guidance (e.g., "What happened next?" or "What else do we need?") is likely to encourage other literacy behavior. One key to the success of implicit instruction is providing feedback so that the child knows he or she was successful (e.g., "You remembered a lot of things that happened at the zoo!" or "You helped Mommy remember all the things we need at the store.").

There is one particularly important thing to remember when encouraging parents to use different kinds of instructional practices as part of their children's participation in everyday literacy learning activities. The goal is to support and encourage literacy learning *naturally* and not turn these activities into formal, highly structured instructional episodes. Doing so can backfire and have negative consequences (Janes & Kermani, 2001).

Summary

This article provided information about the precursors of literacy skills (literacy domains), the everyday activities that provide opportunities for early literacy learning, and the instructional practices that can be used by parents to support and encourage the development of their children's literacy skills. Several models were included to help structure interventions to promote children's participation in early literacy experiences (natural learning environments) in ways that increase the likelihood of the development of specific kinds of literacy competencies. The contents of this article include the ingredients necessary to provide young children the building blocks for successful literacy learning.

The focus of the approach to literacy learning described in this article is the kinds of informal, everyday activities that are the literacy-rich natural learning environments that happen in the context of family and community life. This approach is based on an extensive body of research and practice on how the development of literacy skills is influenced by the opportunities afforded children as part of everyday family and community life. This type of literacy learning reinforces the kinds of learning opportunities provided as part of more formal interventions. The premise of our approach is that more opportunities of the right kind of literacy learning activities can only strengthen the development of literacy competence.

Note

You can reach Carl J. Dunst by e-mail at dunst@puckett.org

References

Anthony, J. L., & Lonigan, C. J. (2004). The nature of phonological awareness: Converging evidence from four studies of preschool and early grade school children. *Journal of Educational Psychology, 96,* 43–55.

Armbruster, B. B., Lehr, F., & Osborn, J. (2003). *Put reading first: The research building blocks for teaching children to read.* Washington, DC: National Institute for Literacy.

Bruder, M. B., Trivette, C. M., Dunst, C. J., & Hamby, D. (2000, December). *Comparative study of natural learning environment interventions to promote English language learning.* Poster presented at the 16th Annual DEC International Early Childhood Conference on Children With Special Needs, Albuquerque, NM.

Cairney, T. H. (2002). Bridging home and school literacy: In search of transformative approaches to curriculum. *Early Child Development and Care, 172,* 153–172.

Dunst, C. J., Bruder, M. B., Trivette, C. M., & Hamby, D. W. (in press). Everyday activity settings, natural learning environments, and early intervention practices. *Journal of Policy and Practice in Intellectual Disabilities.*

Dunst, C. J., Hamby, D., Trivette, C. M., Raab, M., & Bruder, M. B. (2002). Young children's participation in everyday family and community activity. *Psychological Reports, 91*, 875–897.

Dunst, C. J., Hamby, D., Trivette, C. M., Raab, M., & Bruder, M. B. (2000). Everyday family and community life and children's naturally occurring learning opportunities. *Journal of Early Intervention, 23*, 151–164.

Dunst, C. J., Raab, M., & Shue, P. (in press). *Early literacy experiences scale.* Asheville, NC: Winterberry Press.

Dyson, A. H. (2002). Writing and children's symbolic repertoires: Development unhinged. In S. B. Neuman & D. K. Dickinson (Eds.), *Handbook of early literacy research* (pp. 220–241). New York: Guilford.

Janes, H., & Kermani, H. (2001). Caregivers' story reading to young children in family literacy programs: Pleasure or punishment? *Journal of Adolescent and Adult Literacy, 44*, 458–466.

Kaiser, A. P., Hemmeter, M. L., Ostrosky, M. M., Fischer, R., Yoder, P., & Keefer, M. (1996). The effects of teaching parents to use responsive interaction strategies. *Topics in Early Childhood Special Education, 16*, 375–406.

National Institute of Child Health and Human Development. (2000). *Report of the National Reading Panel. Teaching children to read: An evidence-based assessment of the scientific research literature on reading and its implications for reading instruction.* Washington, DC: U.S. Government Printing Office.

Nelson, K. (1999, Winter). Making sense: Language and thought in development. *Developmental Psychologist*, 1–10.

Neuman, S. B., & Dickinson, D. K. (Eds.). (2002). *Handbook of early literacy research.* New York: Guilford.

Neuman, S. B., & Roskos, K. (1993). Access to print for children of poverty: Differential effects of adult mediation and literacy-enriched play settings on environmental and functional print tasks. *American Educational Research Journal, 30*, 95–122.

Pullen, P. C., & Justice, L. M. (2003). Enhancing phonological awareness, print awareness, and oral language skills in preschool children. *Intervention in School and Clinic, 38*, 87–98.

Rome-Flanders, T., Cronk, C., & Gourde, C. (1995). Maternal scaffolding in mother-infant games and its relationship to language development: A longitudinal study. *First Language, 15*, 339–355.

Roskos, K. A., Tabors, P. O., & Lenhart, L. A. (2004). *Oral language and early literacy in preschool.* Newark, DE: International Reading Association.

Seitz, S., & Stewart, C. (1975). Imitations and expansions: Some developmental aspects of mother-child communications. *Developmental Psychology, 11*, 763–768.

Shue, P. L. (2005). Sources of information about preliteracy development. *CASEmakers, 1*(3), 1–4. Retrieved from http://www.fippcase.org/products.

Shue, P., & Dunst, C. J. (in press-a). Everyday family and community contexts of early literacy learning. *CASEinPoint.*

Shue, P., & Dunst, C. J. (in press-b). Sources of information about everyday community literacy activities. *CASEmakers.*

Shue, P., & Dunst, C. J. (in press-c). Sources of information about everyday family literacy activities. *CASEmakers.*

Snow, C. (2002). *Reading for understanding: Toward an R&D program in reading comprehension.* New York: RAND Corp.

Snow, C. E., Burns, M. S., & Griffin, P. (Eds.). (1998). *Preventing reading difficulties in young children.* Washington, DC: National Academy Press.

Strickland, D. S., & Schickedanz, J. A. (2004). *Learning about print in preschool.* Newark, DE: International Reading Association.

Trivette, C. M. (2003). Influence of caregiver responsiveness on the development of young children with or at risk for developmental disabilities. *Bridges, 1*(3), 1–13. Retrieved from http://www.evidencebasedpractices.org/bridges/bridges_vol1_no3.pdf.

Trivette, C. M., Dunst, C. J., & Hamby, D. (2004). Sources of variation in and consequences of everyday activity settings on child and parenting functioning. *Perspectives in Education, 22*(2), 17–35.

Ukrainetz, T. A., Cooney, M. H., Dyer, S. K., Kysar, A. J., & Harris, T. J. (2000). An investigation into teaching phonemic awareness through shared reading and writing. *Early Childhood Research Quarterly, 15*, 331–355.

Whitehurst, G. J., & Lonigan, C. J. (2001). Emergent literacy: Development from prereaders to readers. In S. B. Neuman & D. K. Dickinson (Eds.), *Handbook of early literacy research* (pp. 11–29). New York: Guilford.

A Home Literacy Inventory:

Assessing Young Children's Contexts for Emergent Literacy

Christine A. Marvin, Ph.D., and Nancy J. Ogden, M.A.,
University of Nebraska

Introduction

For most parents, the expectation that their children will become literate is a natural and appropriate assumption. Yet this assumption does not always become a reality. For a variety of reasons, some children may arrive in kindergarten or first grade with limited knowledge of books and stories, may show difficulty recognizing more than their own name in print, and may show a lack of interest and skill in writing or drawing activities. Although some educators and parents would argue that first grade is soon enough for learning reading and writing skills, others would emphasize the importance of ample emergent literacy experiences before first grade. These experiences could include handling and talking about picture books, reciting nursery rhymes, scribbling or early writing, listening to stories told or read by others, talking about past events with adults, and/or identifying familiar logos or names in print. Without such experiences, research indicates a greater possibility of poor reading ability in first grade and later school failure (Dickinson & DeTemple, 1998; Dickinson & Tabors, 1991; Neuman & Dickinson, 2001; Snow, Barnes, Chandler, Goodman, & Hemphill, 1991).

> *For a variety of reasons, some children may arrive in kindergarten or first grade with limited knowledge of books and stories, may show difficulty recognizing more than their own name in print, and may show a lack of interest and skill in writing or drawing activities.*

A number of home/family factors are related to development of emergent literacy skills in preschool-age children. These include family socioeconomic and educational levels (Auerbach, 1989; Heath, 1983; White, 1982), parental aspirations for their children's education (Hiebert & Adams, 1987), and the quality of adult-child interactions at home

(Teale & Sulzby, 1987). More specific factors that have been identified in the literature include:

- Children are read to regularly (Anderson & Stokes, 1984; Heath, 1983)
- Children have the opportunity to read to others (Teale & Sulzby, 1987, 1989)
- Children see others reading for functional purposes (Cochran-Smith, 1984)
- Children have easy access to reading and writing materials (Cochran-Smith, 1984)
- Children are encouraged to discuss stories and characters during reading and writing activities (Hemphill & Snow, 1996; Rush, 1999)
- Children engage in a variety of conversations about past and present events, with and without books, at home (Lonigan & Whitehurst, 1999)
- Children engage in sound-play such as nursery rhymes, finger plays, songs, poems, or stories that contain rhymes, repeated or nonsense sound sequences (Catts, 1991)
- Children watch TV or videos with adults who comment on and explain events, plots, and character motives and actions (Mason, 1980)

These emergent literacy experiences are viewed as applicable to all young children, including those with disabilities and developmental delays (Dale, Crain-Thoreson, Notari-Syverson, & Cole, 1996; Gillam & Johnston, 1985; Katims, 1991; Marvin & Mirenda, 1993). Many young children with disabilities, although often considered at high risk for reading difficulties, have learned to read despite physical and/or cognitive limitations. And although some may never learn to read because of severe cognitive/linguistic impairments, most can acquire at least a functional use of print for receiving and delivering messages for safety, social, and academic purposes. The factors identified as key to their success are similar to those factors described for nondisabled populations. These include familial support and encouragement received in the early years and the opportunities at home and school to view themselves as readers and writers (Brown, 1954; Koppenhaver, Evans, & Yoder, 1991; Rush, 1986; Smith, 1992).

Surveying Home Literacy Experiences

Understanding the emergent literacy environments in which children live can be an important step in a teacher's efforts to design individually appropriate language-literacy experiences for preschool-age children. Parent reports have been the most prevalent approach for examining the home literacy experiences of young children and have been found to be reliable and predictive measures of young children's literacy skills once they begin school (Dickinson & DeTemple, 1998). Simple-to-complete parent surveys have been useful in providing detailed information about children's and adults' behaviors during reading and writing activities at home for various age groups (Watson, Orovitz, & Andrews, 1998) and high risk populations of children (Dickinson & DeTemple, 1998; Light & Kelford-Smith, 1993; Marvin & Mirenda, 1993; McCathren & Allor, 2002). Whereas other instruments are useful in assessing children's specific emergent literacy skills, such as print awareness, phonological awareness, and oral language skills (Clay, 1979; Gardner, 1990; Notari-Syverson, O'Connor, & Vadasay, 1998), or classroom supports (Smith & Dickinson, 2002), parental surveys provide insight into children's current support and contexts for learning about print and sound-letter relationships outside of the formal educational program. This information can be helpful in designing "individualized" language-literacy programs that build on the literacy foundation laid at home.

The "Home Literacy Inventory" presented in this article (see Table 1) was originally developed for a series of studies on the home literacy experiences of young children ages three to six with and without disabilities (Marvin, 1994; Marvin & Gaffney, 1999; Marvin & Mirenda, 1993; Marvin & Wright, 1997). More than 1,000 families successfully completed the printed surveys, including two percent who did not report English to be the primary language used in their home. Overall, the preschool children with disabilities (ages three to six years) presented significantly different home literacy experiences and abilities from a group of Head Start children and a group of nondisabled peers from middle and upper class homes. Within the group of children with disabilities, advantages were noted for children with single vs. multiple disabilities and for those without disabilities vs. those with speech-language impairments.

A Home Literacy Inventory

As teachers collect information about children's motor, cognitive, social, communication, and self-help skills they also should consider the importance of knowing more about the children's emerging literacy skills. The "Home Literacy Inventory" presented can provide useful information about children's emergent literacy abilities and experiences that can shape classroom activities, teacher-child interactions, and home

Table 1

Home Literacy Inventory

Child's Name: _____ Today's Date: _____ Date of Birth: _____ Age: ____

Complete the following items with your child's current interests and abilities in mind. Not all items will apply to your child or your home. Children who are older (4–6 years old) may have more interests and skills than younger children (2–3 years old). Families, too, may differ in their interests and practices with their children. Check only those items that apply to you and your child.

(1) What is your child's favorite:

Storybook?_____
Movie/video?_____
TV show?_____
Nursery rhyme/finger song? _____
Writing/drawing utensil? _____

NONPRINT ACTIVITIES

(2) How does your child watch TV/videos at home? (Check the one that is *most* common):

_____ alone
_____ with other children/adults in the room
_____ with an adult commenting on/ explaining the program

(3) Which of the following nonprint activities does your child do with someone at home *at least weekly?* (Check all that apply):

_____ sings children's songs
_____ does "finger play" songs or games (e.g., Itsy Bitsy Spider, Wheels on the Bus)
_____ recites nursery rhymes, poems, or jingles
_____ tells made-up stories without books
_____ sings the ABCs
_____ listens to stories on audio tapes
_____ plays rhyming games (e.g., dog/ bog, cat/rat, boy/toy, open/ropen)
_____ makes up nonsense words or *pretends* to talk in another language
_____ has fun talking very fast or very slow
_____ tells about events/activities he or she did without you
_____ retells stories heard or seen in videos, movies, TV, or books
_____ finds the first letter of his or her name in logos/commercials & everyday print
_____ spells his or her name or familiar words out loud

READING ACTIVITIES

(4) How frequently do you or other family members read stories/books aloud to your child? (Check one):

_____ less than once a week
_____ 1-2 times each week
_____ daily

(5) Where is your child most often positioned for shared book reading with you at home? (Choose the two most typical positions):

_____ in his or her special chair
_____ at a table
_____ on an adult's lap
_____ beside an adult on sofa, large chair, or floor
_____ lying in bed
_____ other:_____

(6) How frequently does your child "read" or look at books by himself or herself at home? (Check one):

_____ never
_____ at least 1-2 times each week
_____ less than once a week
_____ daily

(7) When you or someone else at home reads a book with your child, what do you usually do? (Check all that apply):

_____ read the title page/cover
_____ tell the story in your own words
_____ read the words in the book
_____ point to page numbers and name them
_____ point to the pictures and label them
_____ point to the words in the book
_____ point to letters and name them
_____ ask your child to "turn the page"
_____ ask your child to label the pictures (e.g., "What's this?")
_____ ask your child to point to the pictures (e.g., "Where is the _____?" "Show me the ___.")
_____ ask your child to point to a word (e.g., "Can you find the word zoo?")
_____ ask your child to read a word (e.g., "What does this say?")
_____ read a word incorrectly and wait for your child to correct you
_____ ask your child what happened in the story
_____ ask your child what will happen next in the story
_____ ask your child to explain why something happened
_____ relate events and characters in the story to your child's own life

(8) How does your child participate during shared reading activities at home? (Check all that apply):

_____ chooses books to read alone or to be read aloud

Table 1 (*continued*)

_____ listens quietly as someone else reads aloud
_____ reads the title/cover
_____ turns pages
_____ reads the page numbers
_____ finds words with the same letters as his or her own name
_____ says "the end" when the story is finished
_____ pretends to read the book
_____ points to pictures
_____ labels pictures of objects and people
_____ labels the action in pictures
_____ asks you questions or makes comments about the story during reading
_____ answers your questions during or after reading
_____ asks you, "What does this say?"
_____ points to and reads familiar words
_____ retells the story while turning the pages
_____ tries to guess what will happen next
_____ other: _____

(9) Which of the following activities does your child do *at least once a month?* (Check all that apply):

_____ visits the library/bookmobile
_____ goes to a bookstore
_____ selects videos for rental
_____ dials a familiar number on the telephone
_____ selects a favorite packaged food at the grocery or convenience store

(10) What printed material does your child *see or use in the home at least weekly?* (Check all that apply):

Sees adults use weekly		Child "looks at" with interest weekly
_____	magazines	_____
_____	novels/other adult books	_____
_____	dictionary/encyclopedia	_____
_____	newspaper	_____
_____	catalogs	_____
_____	advertisement flyers	_____
_____	phone book	_____
_____	letters	_____
_____	TV/movie guide	_____
_____	cookbooks/instruction manuals	_____
_____	photographs of family/friends	_____
_____	checkbook/budget book/bills	_____
_____	comic books	_____
_____	picture books for children	_____
_____	story books for children	_____
_____	notes (refrigerator notes)	_____
_____	birthday cards (on a birthday)	_____
_____	food packages/logos	_____
_____	clocks/watches	_____
_____	logos on clothes	_____
_____	own name on paper or package	_____
_____	other: _____	_____

WRITING ACTIVITIES

(11) How often does your child do some writing, drawing, or "pretend writing" at home? (Check one):

_____ less than once a week
_____ at least once a week
_____ daily

(12) Which of the following writing/drawing materials does your child *see or use at home at least weekly?* (Check all that apply):

Sees adults use weekly		Child uses weekly
_____	pencil/pen & paper	_____
_____	crayons/markers	_____
_____	paintbrushes, paints	_____
_____	chalk	_____
_____	computer	_____
_____	typewriter	_____
_____	calculator	_____
_____	writing/drawing toys	_____
_____	other writing tools	_____

(13) When you or someone else at home draws or writes with your child, *what do you usually do?* (Check all that apply):

_____ position a writing/drawing utensil in the child's hand
_____ provide hand-over-hand assistance
_____ comment on what the child is drawing/writing
_____ sit silently and watch while the child draws/writes
_____ leave the child alone while he or she draws/writes
_____ encourage the child to "draw/write more"
_____ tell the child what to draw/write or which colors to use
_____ encourage the child to copy what you draw/write
_____ write the child's name on the paper
_____ encourage the child to write his or her own name
_____ encourage the child to "pretend" to write
_____ draw/write a model for the child to copy
_____ answer the child's questions
_____ write words the child dictates to you
_____ spell words aloud for the child to write
_____ make the letter sounds for the child to guess and write

(14) When your child is writing or drawing at home, *what does he or she typically do?* (Check all that apply):

_____ chooses writing/drawing activities
_____ draws pictures on paper

Table 1 (*continued*)

_____ draws pictures on a computer	_____ recognizes 5 or more logos (e.g.,
_____ plays with writing and drawing toys	K-Mart, McDonald's, Coke/Pepsi,
(Etch-a-Sketch®, Magna-Doodle®,	Dairy Queen)
etc.)	_____ reads 5 or more sight words (e.g.,
_____ practices writing/typing letters in	stop, exit)
the alphabet	_____ reads 10 or more words in books
_____ copies letters or words	_____ reads 25-50 words
_____ writes his or her name	_____ reads sentences in picture books
_____ pretends to write by scribbling	_____ reads simple stories without pictures
_____ writes words independently	(16) Which one of the following statements
_____ types words independently using a	*best* describes your child's current writing
computer or typewriter	skills? (Check *one*):
_____ dictates words or sentences for oth-	
ers to write down	_____ does not write/draw at all
_____ makes posters or signs for special	_____ scribbles/colors unrecognizable
events	pictures
	_____ colors in coloring books
CHILD'S CURRENT ABILITIES	_____ draws pictures of recognizable
(15) Which one of the following statements	objects and characters
best describes your child's current reading	_____ writes some or all letters in the
skills? (Check *one*):	alphabet
	_____ writes or copies his or her name
_____ does not read at all	_____ writes/copies simple, familiar words
_____ pretends to read	_____ writes simple notes, sentences
_____ recognizes letters of the alphabet	_____ writes simple stories or answers to
	questions

visitation discussions. Adapted from the survey used in the Marvin home literacy studies, the Inventory is not intended to be an evaluation of home environments but an index of children's current and recent past interactions with print and print-related conversations. The Inventory prompts teachers to consider children's: (1) *nonprint activities* such as guided TV viewing, singing songs and rhymes, and sharing of events with adults at home; (2) *reading activities* both with and without an adult; (3) *writing activities*, both independent and adult-supported; and (4) *current reading and writing abilities*. Educators should consider the "Home Literacy Inventory" one small part of the battery of tools used for getting to know individual children prior to designing relevant, individualized educational plans for children three to six years of age.

... [T]he Inventory is not intended to be an evaluation of home environments but an index of children's current and recent past interactions with print and print-related conversations.

The "Home Literacy Inventory" could be completed by parents as a written survey, through structured interview, or open-ended discussion. For example, whether by necessity (i.e., non-native English speaking parent) or by choice, a teacher could engage family members in a discussion of young children's reading and writing interests and opportunities at home. Open-ended questions such as, "Tell me about Maria's interest in books at home" could provide information or lead to follow-up questions that permit checking Inventory items as +/–. Similarly, open-ended questions about children's writing or drawing at home and the adult's role in such activities would permit a teacher to gain information without having to read the questions verbatim. The information on the "Home Literacy Inventory" need not be collected in one sitting or all at one time. For some families and teachers, the collection of the information over a number of days or weeks may be more appropriate and informative.

The "Home Literacy Inventory" was used to guide an interview during two home visits with Maria's family. Maria's mother and father told her ECSE teacher that Maria loves to look at books alone and have books read to her. They indicated that she has a couple books of her own that she received for her birthday and that her older brother and sister will sometimes bring books home from their school, which they can read to Maria. When Maria is looking at books by herself, her parents said she frequently pretends to read them, making up stories about the pictures. Maria also frequently asks to write when she sees one of her parents making grocery lists, writing letters or checks, or making to-do lists. Her parents said they are teaching Maria to write her name with a pen, but currently she only scribbles.

Finally, teachers also may collect some of the information by observation. During home visits, the teacher may take note of print materials available in the home for children and create, during those visits, opportunities for children or adults to write notes, draw pictures, or share storybooks with one another. Such activities could easily lead to a "show and tell" discussion during the visit about typical and favorite literacy experiences for the child, as well as parental aspirations and the subsequent completion of the Inventory with the parent(s).

The ECSE teacher visited Josh's home and the home of his child care provider during October and November as part of an agreement with his family. The teacher observed family magazines and children's books in Josh's home, but not in the child care home. Josh was observed using books as props as he played with other toys (e.g., books lined up to be a road for his cars). Josh was not observed "reading" books, and his mother and child care provider reported that he rarely asks to be read to nor looks at books by himself. They reported that he likes videos better and watches them alone for hours. Josh did have crayons and coloring books at both homes and was observed scribbling in a picture book at home. When asked about books for the children at the child care home, the provider reported that she was afraid the children would just "tear them up."

What to Do With the Information

No total score is computed for the "Home Literacy Inventory." Items positively checked do not correspond to age-specific norms. There are no criteria for how many items a child of a given age or with a particular disability/delay should be experiencing at home. Once an Inventory is completed, however, and a child's home experiences noted, teachers can use the information in conjunction with the results from observations or specific child assessments to develop individualized language-literacy experiences at school (and for home) that reflect the child's current abilities, needs, and experiences, as well as current family practices. For example, it may be necessary for some children to have a literacy program that includes attention to such basic emergent literacy skills as handling books, recognizing a message in print and pictures, identifying beginnings and ends of pages and stories, and scribbling to convey a message (or their name).

... [I]t may be necessary for some children to have a literacy program that includes attention to such basic emergent literacy skills as handling books, recognizing a message in print and pictures, identifying beginnings and ends of pages and stories, and scribbling to convey a message (or their name).

These same children may benefit from opportunities to talk about recent events or be prompted to describe recent activities with and without context clues if they have had limited experience with these types of activities previously. Furthermore, families and care providers may request and benefit from coaching regarding these types of interactions.

Josh was encouraged to hold the book for the teacher at school during read-aloud time. He was introduced to picture books with audio tapes and would sit with an adult to listen to these stories. He liked being in charge of turning the page. The teacher met with the child care provider and offered to co-conduct a book reading activity with all the children at her next visit. The provider was interested in viewing a videotape about reading to young children before the teacher made her next visit. Josh's family indicated interest in having Josh read more at home. They welcomed the idea of a storybook coming home each week from school. The parents were encouraged to invite Josh to "read" the book to them by describing the pictures and have Josh turn pages as they read the book at least once each week to Josh.

For other children, however, time spent on such aspects of emerging literacy would be review and not necessarily developmentally appropriate or interesting. Children who reportedly have daily experience with logos, books, crayons, storytelling, and event sharing at home may benefit from literacy programs that focus more on the letter, sound, or word identification in text, character relationships in stories, oral storytelling, and functions of typed as well as written messages. Even if children are not showing more advanced letter/word recognition skills, the "Home Literacy Inventory" can provide information to clarify whether their emergent literacy experiences are sufficient to support these more advanced skills.

Maria's ECSE teacher instigated a weekly book check-out system using the school library and classroom resources. She planned a Family Night at the local library when families could obtain library cards. Maria's teacher also developed a writing center in her ECSE classroom. She included several types of paper (e.g., lined, unlined, notebooks, tablets), a variety of writing utensils (e.g., large pencils, crayons, and markers), and a typewriter. A small group activity was designed to have the children write thank-you notes to the families who had sent in snack items for the class. During this small group time, some of the children used pretend writing, some copied words written by the teacher, and other children dictated their notes to the paraeducator. All of the notes were duplicated and sent home with each child.

During the next home visit with Maria's family, her mother commented on how surprised she was that so many of the children in Maria's class were writing in some way or another. Maria's teacher had brought paper and writing utensils with her and engaged Maria in a book-making activity about their recent field trip. Maria's teacher demonstrated for Maria's mother how to write what Maria said about the picture that Maria drew on the first page of her book. She had Maria's mother write Maria's words on subsequent pages, and prompted Maria to write her name on the title page and "write" (scribble) a title for the story.

Finally, some children will have histories that include recitation of rhymes and play with nonsense words, as well as frequent reading of storybooks and sharing of recent or past events. These children may already recognize letters in print and be able to spell their own name (orally or in writing). Children with these abilities and experiences could benefit most from a literacy program that moved them into roles of authorship, decoding words and sentences, and reading for everyday purposes. The possibility exists that young children with and without disabilities and of any age (three to six years) can present this full range of emerging literacy skills and require individualized attention to advance their knowledge and skills. In addition, individual families may indicate interest in particular aspects of literacy due to the primary language used in the home and/or cultural traditions. The "Home Literacy Inventory" can highlight those preferences.

Teachers may also use the information collected on the "Home Literacy Inventory" to guide their plans for parent education meetings, open house activities, and family home visits. Teachers could model for families how to interpret the unique (often subtle) cues their children present that indicate an interest in books or drawing and demonstrate strategies for successful reading and writing activities at home for children with sensory or physical disabilities.

Over the past month, Cassidy's mother, father, and ECSE teacher spent part of each home visit completing and discussing the "Home Literacy Inventory." Cassidy's parents and teacher identified the objectives they would address the coming week as the family engaged Cassidy in shared book reading while in their lap or seated in her adaptive chair. Additionally, the use of an audio taped story and picture board of the favorite story was considered a real asset for Cassidy as she was able to point to characters and predict what would happen next as the story was told. Furthermore, upon request, Cassidy could enjoy the story independently or share the taped story with her older brother.

Finally, by designing activities at school that build on the children's past experiences, teachers can share with families specific observations that highlight the progress children have made relative to reading and writing interests. Anecdotal notes of observed literacy activities at school and samples (e.g., video, audio, paper) of children's independent reading or drawing/writing can be included in a child's portfolio to note changes over time and/or to compare with samples family members have collected. The "Home Literacy Inventory" provides a means for engaging family members in a discussion of the importance of emergent literacy activities for young children. Parents may find it easier to include emergent literacy activities within their children's daily lives after becoming familiar with the "Home Literacy Inventory." Repeated discussions about young children's interests and abilities relative to emergent literacy and a repeated completion of the "Home Literacy Inventory" a second time each year ensures that both teachers and family members will maintain emerging literacy activities as a priority for young children.

Summary

Teachers would be well-advised to complete a thorough assessment of both children's emerging literacy skills and their home literacy exper-iences before beginning a literacy development program. The "Home Literacy Inventory" can be a useful tool in teachers' battery of assessments to learn all they can about children's knowledge and experiences with print and language at home. The more infor-mation available to teachers, the more able they will be to design individually appropriate interventions and educa-tional programs. The inclusion of emer-gent literacy activities, at home as well as at school, can have significant impact on the future social and academic success of children, especially for chil-dren with known disabilities and/or developmental delays (Katims, 1991). In addition, the inclusion of information about young children's home literacy experiences may assist teachers in providing services that incor-porate the family's strengths in guiding their children toward literacy.

> *The inclusion of emergent lit-eracy activities, at home as well as at school, can have sig-nificant impact on the future social and academic success of children, especially for children with known disabilities and/or developmental delays....*

Notes
A .PDF version of the "Home Literacy Inventory" is available from the first author. You can reach Christine A. Marvin by e-mail at cmarvin1@unl.edu

References
Anderson, A., & Stokes, S. (1984). Social and institutional influences on the development and practice of literacy. In H. Goelman, A. Oberg, & F. Smith (Eds.), *Awakening to literacy* (pp. 24–37). Exeter, NH: Heinemann Educational Books.
Auerbach, E. (1989). Toward a sociocultural approach to family literacy. *Harvard Educational Review, 59,* 165–181.
Brown, C. (1954). *My left foot.* London: Secker and Warburg.
Catts, H. (1991). Early identification of reading disabilities. *Topics in Language Disorders, 12,* 1–16.
Clay, M. (1979). *The early detection of reading difficulties: A diagnostic survey with recovery procedures* (3rd ed.). Portsmouth, NH: Heinemann Educational Books.
Cochran-Smith, M. (1984). *The making of a reader.* Norwood, NJ: Ablex.
Dale, P., Crain-Thoreson, C., Notari-Syverson, A., & Cole, K. (1996). Parent-child book reading as an intervention for young children with language delays. *Topics in Early Childhood Special Education, 16,* 213–235.
Dickinson, D., & DeTemple, J. (1998). Putting parents in the picture: Maternal reports of preschoolers' literacy as a predictor of early reading. *Early Childhood Research Quarterly, 13,* 241–262.
Dickinson, D., & Tabors, P. (1991). Early literacy: Linkages between home, school, and literacy achieve-ment at age five. *Journal of Research in Childhood Education, 6,* 30–44.
Gardner, M. (1990). *Expressive, one-word picture vocabulary test (Rev.).* Novato, CA: Academic Therapy Press.

Gillam, R., & Johnston, J. (1985). Development of print-awareness in language-disordered preschoolers. *Journal of Speech and Hearing Research, 28,* 521–526.

Heath, S. (1983). *Ways with words: Language, life, and work in communities and classrooms.* New York: Cambridge University Press.

Hemphill, L., & Snow, C. (1996). Language and literacy: Discontinuities and differences. In D. Olson & N. Torrance (Eds.), *The handbook of education and human development: New models of learning, teaching, and schooling* (pp. 173–201). Cambridge: Blackwell.

Hiebert, E., & Adams, C. (1987). Fathers' and mothers' perceptions of their preschool children's emergent literacy. *Journal of Experimental Child Psychology, 44,* 25–37.

Katims, D. (1991). Emergent literacy in early childhood special education: Curriculum and instruction. *Topics in Early Childhood Special Education, 11,* 69–84.

Koppenhaver, D., Evans, D., & Yoder, D. (1991). Childhood reading and writing experiences of literate adults with severe speech and motor impairments. *Augmentative and Alternative Communication, 7,* 20–33.

Light, J., & Kelford-Smith, A. (1993). The home literacy experiences of preschoolers who use augmentative communication systems and of their nondisabled peers. *Augmentative and Alternative Communication, 9*(1), 10–25.

Lonigan, C., & Whitehurst, G. (1999). Relative efficacy of parent and teacher involvement in a shared reading intervention for preschool children from low income backgrounds. *Early Childhood Research Quarterly, 13,* 263–290.

Marvin, C. (1994). Home literacy experiences of preschool children with single and multiple disabilities. *Topics in Early Childhood Special Education, 14,* 436–454.

Marvin, C., & Gaffney, J. (1999). The effects of Reading Recovery on children's home literacy experiences. *Literacy, Teaching, and Learning, 4,* 51–80.

Marvin, C., & Mirenda, P. (1993). Home literacy experiences of preschoolers enrolled in Head Start and special education programs. *Journal of Early Intervention, 17,* 351–367.

Marvin, C., & Wright, D. (1997). Literacy socialization in the homes of preschool children. *Language, Speech, and Hearing Services in the Schools, 28,* 154–163.

Mason, J. (1980). When do children begin to read? An exploration of four-year old children's letter and word reading competencies. *Reading Research Quarterly, 15,* 203–227.

McCathren, R., & Allor, J. (2002). Using storybooks with preschool children: Enhancing language and emergent literacy. *Young Exceptional Children, 5*(4), 3–10.

Neuman, S., & Dickinson, D. (2001). *Handbook of early literacy research.* New York: Guilford.

Notari-Syverson, A., O'Connor, R., & Vadasay, P. (1998). *Ladders to literacy.* Baltimore: Paul H. Brookes.

Rush, K. (1999). Caregiver-child interactions and early literacy development of preschool children from low income environments. *Topics in Early Childhood Special Education, 19,* 3–14.

Rush, W. (1986). *Journey out of silence.* Lincoln, NE: Media Productions and Marketing.

Smith, M. (1992). Reading abilities of nonspeaking students: Two case studies. *Augmentative and Alternative Communication, 8,* 57–66.

Smith, M., & Dickinson, D. (2002). *Early language and literacy classroom observation (ELLCO).* Baltimore: Paul H. Brookes.

Snow, C., Barnes, W., Chandler, J., Goodman, I., & Hemphill, L. (1991). *Unfulfilled expectations: Home and school influences on literacy.* Cambridge: Harvard University Press.

Teale, W., & Sulzby, E. (1987). Access, mediation, and literacy acquisition in early childhood. In D. Wagner (Ed.), *The future of literacy in a changing world* (pp. 173–206). New York: Pergamon.

Teale, W., & Sulzby, E. (1989). *Emergent literacy: Young children learn to read and write.* Newark, DE: International Reading Association.

Watson, L., Orovitz, J., & Andrews, M. D. (1998, December 7). *Survey of preschoolers' emergent literacy environments and skills.* Paper presented at the International Conference of the Division for Early Childhood, Chicago, IL.

White, K. (1982). The relation between socioeconomic status and academic achievement. *Psychological Bulletin, 91,* 461–481.

The Tools of Literacy for Infants and Toddlers

Joanne Knapp-Philo, Ph.D.,
California Institute on Human Services,
Sonoma State University, Camarillo, CA

Angela Notari-Syverson, Ph.D.,
Washington Research Institute, Seattle, WA

Kimberly K. Stice, B.S.,
California Institute on Human Services,
Sonoma State University, Camarillo, CA

Louisa is the caregiver for five-month old Aida, 18-month old Dominick, and two and a half-year old Jasmine. She sits on the floor with Adia in her lap and watches Dominick play with a car on the rug. He says "rrrrrrrr" imitating the engine noise, as he's heard others do when playing with cars. Louisa responds to Dominick, saying "rrrrrr ... look at you rrrrrrun the rrrrrrrace car! Does that sound like what you heard when you and Dad went to the races?" Dominick smiles and nods his head vigorously. Louisa laughs, "Your brother, Joe, makes that sound when he plays with cars too." Dominick continues racing his car making louder and longer "rrrrrrrr" sounds. Aida responds to Louise's comments to Dominick by waving her arms and legs excitedly. Louise remarks, "Well look at you, bouncing around ... bouncing on my knee, buzzing like a bee, arms out like a tree, fun for you and me!" She bounces Aida in her lap as she makes up the rhyme they share. Aida watches Louisa's face intently as she smiles and sings the rhyme and responds with big grins, waving arms, and tilting her head left and right.

Jasmine and her mother come into the room and Louisa says, "Good morning Jasmine and Ms. James. How are you both today?" "Good morning!" Jasmine's mother responds as she hands Louisa the journal they use to update each other. "I wrote a few notes last night. Thank you for keeping me updated on Jasmine's progress with potty training." Jasmine kisses her mother goodbye and looks across the room to a shelf that has pictures of dolls above it. She pushes her walker to the shelf and selects her favorite baby doll. Then she drops to the floor, scoots to Louisa, and leans against her as she hugs the doll. Louisa puts her arm around Jasmine, opens the journal, and *says, "Let's see what this says. Dear Louisa, Jasmine hasn't been eating well at night. For the past week, she'll only eat cheese at dinner. We try to get her to eat other things, but that's all she wants, so that's all she eats. I hope she is eating better for you at lunch." Louisa turns to Jasmine and asks, "You're only eating cheese? Are you a mouse?" Jasmine laughs and says, "Cheese yummy!" Louisa turns back to the journal and Jasmine looks on as Louisa runs her fingers across the lines of text. "She's also doing much better with wearing her glasses. Thank you for making sure she's wearing them when she's moving around." Louisa looks at Jasmine and says, "We keep our glasses on, right?" and Jasmine responds, "Glasses on" and smiles at Louisa.*

Louisa closes the notebook. Dominick, who has been watching and listening, reaches for it. "Do you want to look at a book? Let's find a book with some nice pictures." Louisa reaches for a basket of board books nearby. Dominick takes a book, sits across from Louisa, and turns the pages rapidly. He points to a picture of a bird and says, "burr!" Louisa remarks, "Oh, that blue bird is flying hiiiiiigh in the sky." Dominick responds, "hiiiiiiiigh."

Aida begins to squirm and fuss and Louisa notes that she's ready for a diaper change. As Louisa places Aida on the changing table she talks to her about getting a clean, dry diaper and how she'll feel so much better. Aida waves her arms while on the changing table and watches Louisa's face intently as she has her diaper changed. "Yes, I know, that feels much better, doesn't it?" Louisa comments. Louisa places Aida in her lap as she records the diaper change on Aida's chart. Aida watches Louisa write. "Let's see, what time is it? What does the clock say? It's 9:30 and Aida had a wet diaper." They put the chart and pen away and Louisa suggests they go for a walk to the park. Aida smiles and looks toward her cubby, which prominently displays her picture with her name written below. Jasmine gets her walker and looks to Louisa to help her stand, and Dominick runs to get his coat.

Literacy does not consist merely of reading and writing, rather, it is a multifaceted, complex process that is closely intertwined with knowledge of the world (Freire & Macedo, 1987). We use literacy to gain knowledge, to express ideas, and to make sense of our experiences. Likewise, infants and toddlers use this "mental tool" to enable them to "read" and interpret the world long before they read words.

Well before their first birthday, young children experiment with the use and functions of many, varied literacy tools to help them think about and act on their world (Bodrova & Leong, 1996). These literacy tools include among other things songs, signs, pictures, rhymes, photographs, catalogs, newspapers, word play, billboards, calendars, receipts, gestures, stickers, picture books, magnetic letters, Peek-a-Boo, and drawing and writing utensils (Rosenkoetter & Barton, 2002).

In the opening vignette, Louisa uses a variety of strategies and objects to engage the infants and toddlers with *tools of literacy* in their daily routines—miniature toys, picture books, a notebook, a clock, the diaper chart, photographs, songs, and rhyme. Adults can use virtually everything in the environment that interests a child as a tool of literacy, including a photograph on the refrigerator, a logo on a paper bag, a label or design on an article of clothing, even a stick in the sand (Notari-Syverson, in press). Cultures based on oral traditions rely on tools such as storytelling, music, and movement; while in print-based cultures, children participate in experiences with *tools of literacy* such as picture books, signs and labels, drawing and writing utensils, words, and sounds that help build the foundations for formal reading and writing (Orellana & Hernandez, 1999).

> *Adults can use virtually everything in the environment that interests a child as a tool of literacy, including a photograph on the refrigerator, a logo on a paper bag ....*

Tools of Literacy Framework

This article describes a "Tools of Literacy Framework" (Knapp-Philo et al., 2003a). The Framework is designed to support adults intentionally using a wide variety of literacy tools, thereby providing very young children with increased opportunities to build a broad foundation for their future literacy learning. The "Tools of Literacy Framework" includes the following eight categories of experiences: (1) nurturing relationships; (2) listening and talking; (3) discovering the world through words and experiences; (4) adults modeling the value of literacy; (5) using symbols to communicate meaning; (6) sounds including rhymes, rhythms, and songs; (7) experiences with print and writing; and (8) enjoyable experiences with stories and books.

These categories, like most aspects of a young child's learning, are not mutually exclusive and experiences often cross categories. Figure 1 provides a summary of the tasks associated with each category.

Nurturing Relationships

Caregivers play a critical role in supporting the development of early social, cognitive, and language behaviors that are the foundation for

Figure 1
"Tools of Literacy Framework"

Using the Tools of Literacy

Nurturing relationships
- Respond immediately to infants' early communicative attempts
- Comment on what the child is doing
- Consistently respond to the child so he or she feels safe

Listening and talking
- Listen to young children's gurgles, grunts, gestures, sounds
- Respond to early communications with actions and by giving words to the baby's experiences (e.g., "You want me to pick you up.")
- Encourage children to use new words and expressions

Discovering the world through words and experiences
- Assure that babies experience seeing, hearing, touching, tasting, and feeling objects and people
- Provide a mixtures of novel and familiar opportunities and repeat them often

Adults modeling the value of literacy
- Show children that literacy is valuable by reading and writing in their presence
- Explain your purpose when you read, write, or use the computer (e.g., "I'm reading the menu to decide what to order for lunch.")

Using symbols to communicate meaning
- Use and talk about a variety of symbols, such as: photos, pictures, signs, magazines, newspapers, books, calendars, menus, soft toys, puppets, miniature objects, sand, textures, finger paint, and markers
- Explain the meaning of environmental signs (e.g., "That sign means girls use this bathroom.")

Sounds (rhymes, rhythms, and songs)
- Play sound games with babies by repeating their sounds and then varying the sound slightly
- Sing songs, play with words and sounds, recite nursery rhymes together

Experiences with print and writing
- Provide opportunities for children to explore materials (sand, finger paint, water, rice, food, paper, writing utensils)
- Talk about writing as you do it (e.g., use shopping lists, read recipes, etc.)

Enjoyable experiences with stories and books
- Tell stories about yourself; the child and his or her experiences; your family history; what you've read, seen on television, or at the movies; what happened at work
- "Read" everyday objects with the child (e.g., cereal boxes or magazines)
- Engage in shared conversations about books
- Introduce new words, summarize previous events, discuss predictions, make elaborations, and link ideas to previous experiences during mealtime and when reading

later literacy. The developmental process " … begins in infancy and is an ongoing process in which young children expand and refine their knowledge and use of language largely with the help of facilitating adults" (Strickland & Shanahan, 2004, p. 38).

Caregivers play a critical role in supporting the development of early social, cognitive, and language behaviors that are the foundation for later literacy.

When adults consistently respond immediately to infants' early communicative attempts the infants usually develop secure attachments, intentional communication, and the expectation that their behavior has an effect on the world (Bornstein & Tamis-LeMonda, 1989; Bornstein, Tamis-LeMonda, & Baumwell, 2001; Yoder, Warren, McCathren, & Leew, 1998). Adult responses can be linguistic (e.g., commenting on what the child is doing) and nonlinguistic (e.g., imitating the child's expressions or gestures, smiling, looking), and often vary according to different cultures. Children's development is best supported when adult responses are matched to the children's level of development (DeLoache & Mendoza, 1987), for example when a mother adjusts her responses by providing more information and asking more questions as her young child matures. Indeed, mothers' sensitivity during joint play interactions and their ability to use scaffolding with their young child at age one predicts children's language and phonological awareness at ages three and four (Silven, Niemi, & Voeten, 2002).

Infants and toddlers who have secure relationships with their caregivers are more involved in literacy activities such as picture book reading (Bus & van Ijzendoorn, 1995; Bus, Belsky, van Ijzendoorn, & Crnic, 1997). In addition, the more responsive caregivers are to infants and the more time they spend together in literacy-related activities, the better the children develop phonological awareness skills (Lonigan, Dyer, & Anthony, 1996; Silven et al., 2002).

It is critical for infants and toddlers with disabilities to be surrounded by highly responsive and consistent adults (Knapp-Philo et al., 2003a). Some children give muted cues and their communications may be vague and/or less consistent than other children. Adults, then, need to be highly attuned to each child in order to respond in an appropriate and timely manner.

In the vignette, Louisa demonstrates responsiveness and the ability to scaffold to each child's needs in numerous ways. It is clear that she has a strong, positive relationship with all three children. Louisa responds to Aida's excitement about Dominick's car by bouncing her and making up a rhyming song they both enjoyed. When Louisa learns that Jasmine is eating only cheese, they share a joke about Jasmine being a mouse. She also comforts Jasmine when her mother leaves, putting her arm around her and reading her mother's words to Jasmine to ease the transition. When Dominick wants to "read" the journal, Louisa recognizes and responds to his interest while gently redirecting him to an appropriate book that she knows will interest him. Louisa selects her responses based on each child's current level of development, the situation, and her deep understanding of and relationship with each of the children.

Listening and Talking

Children learn about the world as they hear adults talking and as they learn the words that describe their own experiences. It is essential that adults talk and listen to young children and encourage them to use a variety of words and expressions (Hart & Risely, 1995). Listening to infants and toddlers and responding to their communications encourages them to continue communication. Children who hear and tell stories at home before age four are the most likely to have interest and success in learning to read once they get to school (Wells, 1985).

Vocabulary development (i.e., knowing the meaning of words) is dependent on hearing others use words to describe events and on having experiences that help in understanding what is being said. Vocabulary development is important because the vocabulary size predicts later success at reading (Dickinson, McCabe, Anastasopoulos, Peisner-Feinberg, & Poe, 2003). Silven and colleagues (2002) found that early vocabulary (i.e., at one year of age) predicts phonological awareness (i.e., understanding of rhyming and initial sounds) at age three.

Louisa extends Dominick's vocabulary when she reminds him about going to the races with his Dad, and she waits for his response when she notes that he was making the "rrrrrr" noise because he had learned it from his brother Joe. She extends his vocabulary again when she tells him the bird is flying high in the sky. Louisa "listens to" Aida's nonverbal communication when she squirms, indicating she needs a diaper change. While Aida's communication may not be intentional, over time she learns that Louisa can be counted on to respond when she "tells" her something. In addition, Louisa provides Aida with words that describe her experience ("Yes, I know, that feels much better, doesn't it?").

Infants and toddlers with disabilities also benefit from a wide array of opportunities to listen to and "talk" to others (Knapp-Philo et al., 2003a). Their communications may not be easily understood, so adults need to make a conscious effort to recognize and respond to each communication. As children grow, it is often useful to introduce sign language, PECS (Picture Exchange Communication System), and other systemized substitutes for spoken language. Augmenting spoken language in this way gives children, and the adults in their lives, the opportunity to develop an understanding of the give and take of communication, to develop vocabulary, and to express their thoughts and feelings long before they are able to use words for the same purposes.

Discovering the World Through Words and Experiences

Children develop an increasingly complex understanding of the world as they gain experiences and make new neural connections as a result (Shore, 1997). Seeing, hearing, touching, tasting, and feeling objects and people helps infants understand what things are, what they do, and how things differ (e.g., toy car vs. a block, balloon vs. a ball, and mother vs. a stranger) (Barton & Brophy-Herb, in press). Infants and toddlers learn best about literacy through everyday life activities that integrate different developmental domains including cognitive, language, socio-emotional, and fine and gross motor development (Burns, Griffin, & Snow, 1999).

Seeing, hearing, touching, tasting, and feeling objects and people helps infants understand what things are, what they do, and how things differ ....

Children's background knowledge is key to their ability to read successfully (Anderson & Pearson, 1984; Bransford & Johnson, 1972). This is especially important to consider when children have disabilities (Knapp-Philo et al., 2003a). Children with physical disabilities, for example, often do not have the same experiences as more mobile children who creep away from their caregivers, explore what they find, and then creep back on their own. In these instances, some children with physical disabilities may miss a variety of opportunities for learning that more mobile children enjoy. Infants and toddlers who are frequently ill may simply have fewer opportunities than their peers to go places and do things. For a variety of reasons, it is often difficult for families to take infants and toddlers with disabilities to the grocery store, to big brother's soccer games, etc. This difficulty in accessing a variety of community settings, too, results in fewer opportunities for children to gather information, to interact with a rich array of environments that support learning, and to learn new vocabulary from adults. Children whose sensory impairments are not diagnosed or intervened upon shortly after birth are often not able to maximize their experiences because they do not yet have the needed supports that would enable them to do so.

Therefore, when appropriate, adults must be particularly vigilant in their efforts to provide a wide variety of daily experiences to infants and toddlers with disabilities and to repeat those experiences frequently so the children are comfortable and can learn from the repetition.

Louisa uses daily experiences in the child care environment to support the children's language and literacy development. She also provides them with opportunities to experience a variety of community environments. Visiting near-by parks, taking walks in the neighborhood, and going to a store within walking distance, all provide safe, familiar places where infants and toddlers can practice new words and ideas, and extend them when they are ready. In addition, such environments almost always have some novelty (e.g., a dog walking down the street, a bird or plane flying by, a piece of trash to throw away, or leaves that change color in the fall).

Adults Modeling the Value of Literacy

Caregivers help children integrate new experiences with the concepts, ideas, conventions, and language of their culture by modeling, encouraging, providing meaning to activities, giving directions, or adapting materials so that they are appropriate for the children's interest and developmental levels (Klein, 1996; Rogoff, 1993). Modeling is particularly powerful. One of the strongest influences on a child's later literacy development is parental involvement in everyday language and literacy-related activities (Snow, 1993). It is important that children see literacy as a family value and learn early that reading and writing are pleasurable and important (Paratore, Melzi, & Krol-Sinclair, 1999). Families need to weave literacy interactions for many purposes into the fabric of their lives because there is a significant correlation between the home literacy environment and a child's language abilities (Beals, DeTemple, & Dickinson, 1994; Snow, 1993). Adults should model reading, writing, using computers and other technologies, and explain their purposes (e.g., "I'm reading the menu to decide what to order for lunch," "I'm writing down Auntie's new phone number so I'll know what numbers to dial," "I'm e-mailing Grandpa these pictures so he can see what we did on your birthday") (Notari-Syverson, in press).

In the vignette, Louisa and Ms. James talk about what Ms. James has written in the notebook and then Louisa continues to read and talk about it after Ms. James leaves. Jasmine learns that there is meaning in what her mother has written and that it is important to both her mother and Louisa. She sees Louisa run her finger along the lines of the text. Louisa reads the words to her and talks about what she is and is not eating at home. This experience shows Jasmine that written words recall past events and bring information across environments.

Some children with disabilities may need adults to be more explicit and to slow down in order to profit from adult modeling. Instead of completing a task, the adult may say, "I'm writing a list of what we need at the store. Do you want to see my list?" Returning to the list when they get to the store provides the opportunity to reinforce the print experience. "Remember when we made that list? Let's look at it to see what we need to buy. ... Now, it's time to pay for the groceries. Let's look at the list to be sure we got it all. Did we get milk? ... bread?"

Using Symbols to Communicate Meaning

Literacy involves using symbols to communicate and assign meaning. A symbol is an object, word, gesture, sound, or image that stands for something else. Mastering the symbols of their culture is a central developmental task for young children (DeLoache, 1997). Children gradually acquire an ability to use symbols as they interpret and then create initially iconic (e.g., the toy truck represents real ones) and then graphic representations (e.g., "That is a picture of Mommy") (Snow, Burns, & Griffin, 1998). As they become more sophisticated children use a variety of verbal, gestural, and graphic symbols to represent objects, ideas, and feelings and begin to master rule-governed communication systems based on verbal, gestural, and graphic modalities such as spoken English and written text (Wetherby, Warren, & Reichle, 1998).

Children use early symbolic activities to build bridges to literacy (Dyson, 1988), therefore, it is important that adults provide a range of different types of symbols to build the concept that there are multiple tools and modalities for representing objects and ideas. A variety of symbols and literacy tools—photos, pictures, signs, magazines, newspapers, books, calendars, menus, soft toys, puppets, miniature objects, as well as art/drawing tools including sand, textures, finger paint, and markers—should be present and used in homes and child care settings. Such materials should be available throughout the environment (e.g., in the block, pretend play, eating, toileting, and outdoors areas as well as the book and art areas). Louisa puts Aida's picture and name on her cubby so she can learn to associate these symbols with the place where her own personal things are kept.

Symbols play an important role in both cognitive and emotional development (Notari-Syverson, in press). A child's special blanket or teddy bear has personal emotional meaning and is a powerful tool to help the child master the anxiety of being separated from his or her parents and transition to greater independence. For example, Louisa uses the notebook that Jasmine's mother has written in to comfort Jasmine when her mother leaves.

Symbols also are a source of information. Louisa learns about Jasmine eating nothing but cheese from the notebook. Adults help children understand the meaning of signs in the environment by explaining what the pictures tell us (e.g., "That sign means girls use this bathroom."). Louisa shows Aida that the clock has meaning when she "reads" it and marks the time on the diaper chart.

Adults may need to engage in prolonged, intentional planning to support children with cognitive and sensory challenges, since they may need a longer period of time to develop symbolic understanding. In such instances, it is important to provide multiple examples, contexts, and opportunities. It is often helpful to use a variety of kinds of symbols in order to help the child make the connection between the symbol and the object it represents. New experiences should be provided along with familiar ones. Adults can encourage children to learn about the representational nature of symbols with mirrors, photos of the children in the class, and tactile books made from objects gathered by the children.

Sounds (Rhymes, Rhythms, and Songs)

There is a strong relationship between the child's ability to distinguish units of sound and later reading performance during the school years (Ehri & Wilce, 1980; Shankweiler, Crain, Katz, & Fowler, 1995). Most infants use sounds to engage adults from a very early age. When babies coo and babble, adults respond with eye contact, touching, picking them up, hugging them, and matching their sounds to create "conversations." This sound play may be the beginning of the development of phonological awareness (Griffin, in press). Songs and early games with actions and language play are also important culturally-specific tools that help develop later literacy skills. Singing songs, playing with words and sounds, and reciting nursery rhymes all help children develop phonological sensitivity, or sensitivity to the sounds of language. As they play with words and sounds, infants and toddlers discover that words are made up of individual sounds so that when the sound changes the word changes meaning (e.g., "Row, row, row your boat" becomes "Bow, bow, bow your coat!").

As they play with words and sounds, infants and toddlers discover that words are made up of individual sounds so that when the sound changes the word changes meaning ....

Louisa makes up a rhyming song and movements to share with Aida, encourages Dominick to "rrrrrun" his "rrrrrace car," and reminds Dominick that the bird flies "hiiiiiigh" in the sky. Adults can imitate babbling, introduce new sounds, sing songs and nursery rhymes, and encourage children to sing along, fill in parts, play with words, add or change sounds, invent silly words, and talk about how some words sound the same (i.e., rhyme) (Knapp-Philo et al., 2003b).

Songs and music can be powerful tools for many children with disabilities (Kimura, in press). They foster joy and fun, provide children opportunities to practice vocalizing and to move to a beat, and develop vocabulary. Kimura notes that children with hearing loss can feel the vibrations, beat, and rhythm from musical instruments and that children with visual disabilities can sing and dance to music when caring adults provide a safe and supportive environment. Finally, she suggests that infants and toddlers with sensory disorders might prefer soft music or a generalized chant rather than more complex compositions.

Experiences With Print and Writing

Children develop their ability to see meaning in print over time. Infants begin with sensorimotor exploration of materials, toddlers by using their fingers to make marks on paper with finger paint or to trace lines and circles in sand or in their food, for example. They experiment with crumpling or tearing up paper, or exploring with a pencil by banging it on the paper and even making accidental marks. Over time, children who are exposed to print utensils learn how to hold crayons, markers, and paintbrushes; begin to scribble over the page and make dots, lines, and circles; and later draw simple figures and letter-like forms (Dyson, 2000; Ferreiro & Teberosky, 1982). Around age 30 months, children often begin to display their understanding of what writing is about by using it in pretend play to "write orders," "pay checks," and "make lists" (Neuman & Roskos, 1992). By age three most children in the US recognize the golden arches that represent McDonald's restaurant (Snow et al., 1998).

Vukelich (1991) noted that the combination of a literacy-enriched environment and adult mediation increases children's knowledge of writing. Children learn the power and function of print as they observe and interact with literate adults who write, use shopping lists, or use recipes (Clay, 1966). Indeed, young children interact more with print when an adult, providing guidance, makes explicit references to labels, signs, and symbols and provides specific purposes and opportunities for using symbols and literacy tools (Neuman & Roskos, 1992; Vukelich, 1994).

Early experiences with artistic media also can help young children begin to understand and use graphic symbols to express meaning (Dyson, 2000). Adults should encourage infants and toddlers to notice and explore a wide variety of media and model drawing, writing, and painting. Louisa engages Aida as she writes on the diaper chart, talking to her and telling her what she is writing as she does it. She also draws Jasmine's attention to the words her mother has written in the notebook by running her finger along the lines of words as she reads them. This enables Jasmine to see that the written words have meaning—indeed, she learns that the writing is about her!

It is essential that adults not allow their own perceptions of a child's literacy abilities and potential to influence the child's degree of exposure to print and other literacy experiences (Pierce, in press). As with other aspects of literacy, infants and toddlers with disabilities should have the same opportunities to interact with literacy materials in a literacy-rich environment as children without disabilities. Print and other graphic symbols may eventually become a medium through which the child communicates (e.g., in writing, or through augmentative communication systems utilizing pictures or other symbol systems). Some adaptations and accommodations that may provide children with disabilities access to print include: (1) selecting books that are simple and not visually "busy," (2) outlining pictures with dark markers to enhance the discrimination, (3) using enlarged print or magnifying devices, and (4) enhancing the print or pictures with fabric or "puffy" paint to allow for additional tactile information (Lilly & Green, 2004; Pierce & McWilliam, 1993).

Enjoyable Experiences With Stories and Books

Throughout history elders have shared stories with children in order to pass on information about how to function in the world and provide a sense of belonging to the culture. Whether a part of a predominantly print-based or oral-based cultural tradition, many of us hold fond memories of adults sharing stories with us at a tender age. This kind of activity is associated with strong emotional bonds as well as joy, wonder, and awe mixed with a sense of safety and security (Bus, van Ijzendoorn, & Pellegrini, 1995). Early shared picture book reading experiences play this same role, and help children develop emergent literacy and later reading skills that they will need to function in modern society. Such experiences also provide a collaborative context in which adults support children's learning, motivation, and sense of self (DeLoache & Mendoza, 1987; Justice & Kaderavek, 2002).

Reading aloud to children is one of the most important activities for building the skills necessary for independent reading including word knowledge, an understanding of the meaning of print, and awareness of written letters and words (Adams, 1990; Senechal, LeFevre, Thomas, & Daley, 1998). Dialogic reading, in which adults and children engage in a shared conversation about the book, rather than reading it word-for-word, is a powerful way to enhance children's language development (Lonigan & Whitehurst, 1998). Indeed, when adults introduce new words, summarize previous events, make predictions, discuss elaborations, and link ideas to previous experiences during mealtime and when reading, children do better later in reading than when caregivers simply read the words in the book (Beals et al., 1994).

The affective component of sharing stories and books must not be overlooked as it enables young children to build a positive disposition towards literacy (Child Care Action Campaign, 2001). As noted previously, children derive the value of literacy activities early on from the activities that are part of their daily interactions (Paratore, Melzi, & Krol-Sinclair, 1999). This fact is important because while sharing books with babies has many positive benefits, it may not always be the first, best approach with every family. When caregivers are not comfortable or confident about their own literacy skills, they may be better able to support the child's emerging literacy skills by telling stories, or "reading" cereal boxes or magazines together. Such stress-free settings enable adults and children to share positive literacy experiences. As time goes by, and the adults become more confident in their ability to support their child's literacy, they may be able to progress to sharing picture books. It is critical that professionals respect each family's comfort level in this regard, even as they work towards supporting them to eventually engage in more print-based literacy activities with their children (Knapp-Philo et al., 2004).

In the vignette, Louisa uses the notebook as a way to engage Jasmine in a discussion about her not eating and a reminder to wear her glasses. She embraces Jasmine as they read together just after Ms. James leaves. When Dominick wants a book, Louisa has one readily at hand, gives it to him, and encourages his engagement in the book by adding to his labeling of the picture of the bird.

Several studies have shown that at home and in preschool settings children with significant disabilities are offered fewer literacy-related opportunities than their typically developing peers (Marvin, 1994; Marvin & Mirenda, 1993). Coleman-Pierce (1991) reported that preschool teachers believed that two- and three-year olds with significant disabilities were "not ready" for books and crayons, or to participate in storybook reading. It is essential, then, that family members and professionals engage infants and toddlers in story sharing as often as possible. Each child's unique needs should be considered by making sure the child can hold the book, for example, and ensuring that the book is placed in view of the child's gaze (Pierce, in press). Some children with visual impairments will benefit from a clear description of what is happening as adults proceed through the process of reading (e.g., "I am going to turn the page now. Do you want to help me turn the page? We can turn together!").

Conclusion

The "Tools of Literacy Framework" is a useful organizational tool for early childhood and early intervention staff (Knapp-Philo et al., 2003b). The Framework can be used to support systematic and intentional adult-child interactions and can be easily incorporated into ongoing practices because it enables family members and practitioners to review the experiences they are providing and to vary and broaden the number and the kinds of beginning language and literacy opportunities they provide for infants and toddlers. Finally, the *tools of literacy* emerge from day-to-day activities and routines and provide enjoyable experiences for infants, toddlers, and adults.

> ... *[T]he* tools of literacy *emerge from day-to-day activities and routines and provide enjoyable experiences for infants, toddlers, and adults.*

Note
You can reach Joanne Knapp-Philo by e-mail at Joanne.Knapp-Philo@csuci.edu

References
Adams, M. J. (1990). *Beginning to read: Thinking and learning about print*. Cambridge: MIT Press.
Anderson, R. C., & Pearson, P. D. (1984). A schema-thematic view of basic processes in reading comprehension. In P. D. Pearson, R. Barr, M. L. Kamil, & P. Mosenthal (Eds.), *Handbook of reading research* (pp. 255–291). New York: Longman.
Barton, L. R., & Brophy-Herb, H. E. (in press). The developing child from birth to three years: Foundations for language and literacy. In S. E. Rosenkoetter & J. Knapp-Philo (Eds.), *Learning to read the world: Language and literacy in the first three years*. Washington, DC: Zero to Three Press.
Beals, D. E., DeTemple, J. M., & Dickinson, D. K. (1994). Talking and listening that support early literacy development of children from low-income families. In D. K. Dickinson (Ed.), *Bridges to literacy: Children, families, and schools* (pp. 19–40). Cambridge: Blackwell Publishers.
Bodrova, E., & Leong, D. (1996). *Tools of the mind: The Vygotskian approach to early childhood education*. Englewood Cliffs, NJ: Prentice Hall.
Bornstein, M. H., & Tamis-LeMonda, C. S. (1989). Habituation and maternal encouragement of attention in infancy as predictors of toddler language, play, and representational competence. *Child Development, 60*, 738–751.
Bornstein, M. H., Tamis-LeMonda, C. S., & Baumwell, L. (2001). Maternal responsiveness and children's achievement of language milestones. *Child Development, 72*, 748–767.
Bransford, J. D., & Johnson, M. K. (1972). Contextual prerequisites for understanding: Some investigations of comprehension and recall. *Journal of Verbal Learning and Verbal Behavior, 11*, 717–726.

Burns, S., Griffin, P., & Snow, C. (Eds.). (1999). *Preventing reading difficulties in young children.* Washington, DC: National Academy Press.

Bus, A., & van Ijzendoorn, M. (1995). Mothers reading to their 3-year olds: The role of mother-child attachment security in becoming literate. *Reading Research Quarterly, 30,* 998–1015.

Bus, A., Belsky, J., van Ijzendoorn, M., & Crnic, K. (1997). Attachment and bookreading patterns: A study of mothers, fathers, and their toddlers. *Early Childhood Research Quarterly, 12,* 81–98.

Bus, A. G., van Ijzendoorn, M. H., & Pellegrini, A. D. (1995). Joint book reading makes for success in learning to read: A meta-analysis on intergenerational transmission of literacy. *Review of Educational Research, 65,* 1–21.

Child Care Action Campaign. (2001). *Talk, reach, read.* New York: Author.

Clay, D. M. (1966). *Emergent reading behavior.* Auckland, New Zealand: University of Auckland Library.

Coleman-Pierce, P. (1991). *Literacy lost: A qualitative analysis of early literacy opportunities for children with severe speech and physical impairments.* Chapel Hill, NC: University of North Carolina.

DeLoache, J. (1997). Shrinking trolls and expanding minds: How very young children learn to understand and use symbols. *Zero to Three, 17*(3), 10–16.

DeLoache, J. S., & Mendoza, O. (1987). Joint picturebook interactions of mothers and 1-year old children. *British Journal of Developmental Psychology, 5,* 111–123.

Dickinson, D., McCabe, A., Anastasopoulos, L., Peisner-Feinberg, E., & Poe, M. (2003). The comprehensive language approach to early literacy: The interrelationships among vocabulary, phonological sensitivity, and print knowledge among preschool-aged children. *Journal of Educational Psychology, 95,* 465–481.

Dyson, A. H. (2000). Writing and children's symbolic repertoires: Development unhinged. In S. B. Neuman & D. K. Dickinson (Eds.), *Handbook of early literacy research* (pp. 126–141). New York: Guilford.

Dyson, A. H. (1988). Appreciate the drawing and dictating of young children. *Young Children, 43*(3), 25–32.

Ehri, L. C., & Wilce, L. S. (1980). The influence of orthography on readers' conceptualization of the phonemic structure of words. *Applied Psychlinguistics, 1,* 371–385.

Ferreiro, E., & Teberosky, A. (1982*). Literacy before schooling.* Exeter, NH: Heinemann.

Freire, P., & Macedo, D. (1987). *Literacy: Reading the word and reading the world.* Westport, CT: Bergin & Garvey.

Griffin, A. (in press). Phonology: Form in language and literacy. In S. E. Rosenkoetter & J. Knapp-Philo (Eds.), *Learning to read the world: Language and literacy in the first three years.* Washington, DC: Zero to Three Press.

Hart, B., & Risley, T. (1995*). Meaningful differences in the everyday experience of young American children.* Baltimore: Paul H. Brookes.

Justice, L., & Kaderavek, J. (2002). Using shared storybook reading to promote emergent literacy. *Teaching Exceptional Children, 34*(4), 8–13.

Kimura, L. (in press). Music: The great organizer for early language and literacy. In S. E. Rosenkoetter & J. Knapp-Philo (Eds.), *Learning to read the world: Language and literacy in the first three years.* Washington, DC: Zero to Three Press.

Klein, P. S. (1996). *Early intervention: Cross-cultural experiences with a mediational approach.* New York: Garland Publishing.

Knapp-Philo, J., Stice, K., Cole, K., Lim, Y. S., Notari-Syverson, A., Rosenkoetter, S., Saceda, R, Turbiville, V., & Zukoski, A. (2003a). *StoryQUEST 1: Celebrating beginning language and literacy.* Camarillo, CA: California Institute on Human Services, Sonoma State University.

Knapp-Philo, J., Stice, K., Cole, K., Lim, Y. S., Notari-Syverson, A., Rosenkoetter, S., & Zukoski, A. (2003b). *StoryQUEST 2: Celebrating beginning language and literacy.*Camarillo, CA: California Institute on Human Services, Sonoma State University.

Knapp-Philo, J., Stice, K., Lim, Y. S., Notari-Syverson, A., Turbiville, V., & Zukoski, A. (2004). *StoryQUEST 3: Celebrating beginning language and literacy.* Camarillo, CA: California Institute on Human Services, Sonoma State University.

Lilly, E., & Green, C. (2004). *Developing partnerships with families through children's literature.* Upper Saddle River, NJ: Pearson/Prentice-Hall.

Lonigan, C. J., Dyer, S. M., & Anthony, J. L. (1996, April). *The influence of the home literacy environment on the development of literacy skills in children from diverse racial and economic backgrounds.* Paper presented at the Annual Convention of the American Educational Research Association, New York, NY.

Lonigan, C. J., & Whitehurst, G. J. (1998). Relative efficacy of parent and teacher involvement in a shared-reading intervention for preschool children from low-income backgrounds. *Early Childhood Research Quarterly, 13,* 263–292.

Marvin, C. (1994). Home literacy experiences of children with single and multiple disabilities. *Topics in Early Childhood Special Education, 14,* 436–454.

Marvin, C., & Mirenda, P. (1993). Home literacy experiences of preschoolers enrolled in Head Start and in special education programs. *Journal of Early Intervention, 17*, 351–367.

Neuman, S., & Roskos, K. (1992). Literacy objects as cultural tools: Effects on children's literacy behaviors in play. *Reading Research Quarterly, 27*, 203–225.

Notari-Syverson, A. (in press). Everyday tools of literacy. In S. E. Rosenkoetter & J. Knapp-Philo (Eds.), *Learning to read the world. Language and literacy in the first three years*. Washington, DC: Zero to Three Press.

Orellana, M., & Hernandez, A. (1999). Talking the walk: Children reading urban environmental print. *The Reading Teacher, 52*, 612–619.

Paratore, J., Melzi, G., & Krol-Sinclair, B. (1999). *What can we expect of family literacy? Experiences of Latino children whose parents participated in an intergenerational literacy project*. Newark, DE: International Reading Association.

Pierce, P. (in press). Learning to read: High expectations for language and literacy with infants and toddlers with significant disabilities. In S. E. Rosenkoetter & J. Knapp-Philo (Eds.), *Learning to read the world: Language and literacy in the first three years*. Washington, DC: Zero to Three Press.

Pierce, P., & McWilliam, P. (1993). Emerging literacy and young children with severe speech and physical impairments: Issues and possible intervention strategies. *Topics in Language Disorders, 13*(2), 47–57.

Rogoff, B. (1993). Children's guided participation and participatory appropriation in socio-cultural activity. In R. H. Wozniak & K. W. Fischer (Eds.), *Development in context: Acting and thinking in specific environments* (pp. 121–153). Hillsdale, NJ: Lawrence Erlbaum.

Rosenkoetter, S., & Barton, L. (2002). Bridges to literacy: Early routines that promote later school success. *Zero to Three, 22*(4), 33–38.

Senechal, M., LeFevre, J., Thomas, E., & Daley, K. E. (1998). Differential effects of home literacy experiences on the development of oral and written language. *Reading Research Quarterly, 13*, 96–116.

Shankweiler, D., Crain, S., Katz, L., & Fowler, A. E. (1995). Cognitive profiles of reading-disabled children: Comparison of language skills in phonology, morphology, and syntax. *Psychological Science, 6*(3), 149–156.

Shore, R. (1997). *Rethinking the brain: New insights into early development*. Washington, DC: Family and Work Institute.

Silven, M., Niemi, P., & Voeten, M. J. (2002). Do maternal interaction and early language predict phonological awareness in 3- to 4-year olds? *Cognitive Development, 17*, 1133–1155.

Snow, C. E. (1993). Families as social contexts for literacy development. *New Directions for Child Development, 61*, 11–24.

Snow, C., Burns, S., & Griffin, P. (1998). *Preventing reading difficulties in young children*. Washington, DC: National Academy Press.

Strickland, D. S., & Shanahan, T. (2004). Laying the groundwork for literacy. *Educational Leadership, 61*(6), 74–77.

Vukelich, C. (1994). Effects of play interventions on young children's reading of environmental print. *Early Childhood Research Quarterly, 9*, 153–170.

Vukelich, C. (1991). Materials and modeling: Promoting literacy during play. In J. F. Christie (Ed.), *Play and early literacy development* (pp. 215–231). Albany, NY: State University of New York Press.

Wells, C. G. (1985). Preschool literacy-related activities and success in school. In D. Olson, M. Torrance, & A. Hildyard (Eds.), *Literacy, language, and learning* (pp. 18–35). London: Cambridge University Press.

Wetherby, A., Warren, S., & Reichle, J. (1998). *Transitions in prelinguistic communication*. Baltimore: Paul H. Brookes.

Yoder, P., Warren, S., McCathren, R., & Leew, S. (1998). Does adult responsivity to child behavior facilitate communication development? In A. Wetherby, S. Warren, & J. Reichle (Eds.), *Transitions in prelinguistic communication* (pp. 39–58). Baltimore: Paul H. Brookes.

Practical Strategies for Supporting Emergent Literacy in the Preschool Classroom

Mary Louise Hemmeter, Ph.D.,
Jeanette McCollum, Ph.D., and
Wu-Ying Hsieh, Ph.D.,
University of Illinois at Urbana Champaign

Ms. Gillian's preschool classroom in Valley View Elementary School has 18 children including three children with disabilities. The school district has identified emergent literacy as a focus for the district pre-school program for the coming school year. Ms. Gillian already uses the Creative Curriculum and does not want to adopt a specific literacy curriculum. She is eager to learn about strategies she can use to focus on children's emergent literacy in the context of the ongoing activities and routines of the classroom.

The process of becoming literate, of being able to understand and employ the written symbols of the culture, begins very early, well before a child begins formal schooling (Bowman, Donovan, & Burns, 2001; Lyon, 2002). Recently, more attention has been given to emergent literacy, to how literacy develops over time as young children acquire language, learn about their world, come to understand the functions of print, and develop a love of books. Much is now known about emergent literacy, including the skills that children must develop and the environments and strategies that support development of these skills (IRA/NAEYC, 1998). It is clear that children who are at risk for becoming poor readers can, through good teaching, develop a solid foundation in literacy that will enable them to move successfully into kindergarten and the primary grades.

It is clear that children who are at risk for becoming poor readers can, through good teaching, develop a solid foundation in literacy that will enable them to move successfully into kindergarten and the primary grades.

The purpose of this article is to describe: (1) emergent literacy skills that should be addressed during the preschool years, (2) strategies for teaching many of these skills, and (3) practical ideas for embedding the strategies into classroom routines and activities.

What Are Emergent Literacy Skills?

Emergent literacy is *not* reading readiness. Rather, it is a continual process that occurs over time in concert with, and intertwined with, other aspects of development (Notari-Syverson, O'Connor, & Vadasy, 1998). Emergent literacy includes the development of skills, knowledge, and attitudes that provide the foundation for conventional forms of reading and writing (Burns, Griffin, & Snow, 1999). A number of literacy experts have developed early learning outcomes, including outcomes related to emergent literacy (e.g., Neuman, Copple, & Bredekamp, 2000; Snow, Burns, & Griffin, 1998; USDOE, 2001; Whitehurst & Lonigan, 2001). A synthesis of these outcomes is provided in Table 1.

Having a disability may place young children at risk for not developing emergent literacy skills over and above the effects of the disability itself. For example, even though print materials may be available in the home, children with disabilities may have fewer opportunities to participate in literacy-based activities than do their peers (Marvin & Wright, 1997), simply because literacy may not be a high priority when families

Table 1
Emergent Literacy Outcomes

• Excitement and Love of Language and Print Materials

• Comprehension and Meaning From Print Materials
  – Vocabulary
  – Conceptual knowledge
  – Comprehension and use of narrative forms such as descriptions, explanations, and story lines
  – Schemas for participating through words in literacy events, including listening, talking, explaining, and questioning

• Phonological Awareness: The Ability to Hear, Identify, and Manipulate the Sound Structure of Oral Language
  – Phonemic awareness: recognizing that words are divided into a sequence of sounds or phonemes
  – Phonics: connecting oral language with print, and particular sounds with particular written letters

• Alphabetic Principle: Understanding That Particular Letters Are Used to Represent Specific Sounds

have more immediate goals to think about (e.g., stabilizing their child's health, helping the child learn to walk or talk) (Light & Kelford-Smith, 1993; Marvin, 1995). Similarly, early childhood special education as a field may not have heretofore placed a high priority on emergent literacy because our attention has been focused on developmental concerns. New research on emergent literacy, however, provides information that is important for all children by demonstrating the early relationship between development and early literacy skills (e.g., National Reading Panel, 2000). The principle of access to the general education curriculum contained in the IDEA (1997), coupled with research on the strong predictive association between early and later literacy, also underline the critical importance of giving emergent literacy a prominent role in the education of all children, including those with disabilities.

Intervention studies indicate that the development of emergent literacy skills can be influenced through intervention (National Reading Panel, 2000). In addition, these changes often carry over into learning to read (Whitehurst & Lonigan, 2001). Many states have drafted Early Learning Standards that include language arts benchmarks related to a range of early literacy outcomes (e.g., comprehension of text, phonological skills, print awareness). Nevertheless, early childhood educators are just beginning to recognize that it is necessary to think about and provide specifically planned literacy-related opportunities (Snow et al., 1998). Some teachers may question how they can include such a focus within the context of a developmentally appropriate curriculum. Because a focus on emergent literacy is new, many teachers also may not have learned ways to plan opportunities for children to gain these skills or to embed practices supportive of emergent literacy development into their ongoing interactions with children.

Contexts for Supporting Emergent Literacy

One approach to helping educators integrate these important teaching skills is through adoption of an emergent literacy curriculum. A second approach, preferred by Ms. Gillian in the vignette at the beginning of this article, is to embed specific literacy teaching strategies into the current curriculum of the classroom. In this approach, teachers examine their own classroom environments, activities, routines, practices, and interactions, and then develop plans to modify these aspects of their teaching to include more of the practices that have been shown to be related to young children's literacy learning. This is the approach described in this article, and is accomplished through careful attention to designing environments that support literacy learning, planning specific activities that address different emergent literacy outcomes, and using teaching strategies that increase opportunities for learning.

Designing the Environment

The physical environment can be structured to support literacy learning through the strategic use of books, print, and writing materials. Place books throughout the room and guide their placement by matching the context to the book's content. For example, a book about bugs is placed in the science area and a fantasy book is placed in the dramatic play area. Ensure that print that is meaningful to children is readily visible throughout the room (e.g., names on cubbies, labels on shelves, children's dictation on art, picture schedule with labels, class rules with pictures and words). Provide writing materials in relevant areas of the classroom (e.g., envelopes, stamps, pens/pencils, and stationary in a post office dramatic play area). Furthermore, make available a range of books that help children learn about concepts as well as sounds and rhymes.

The social environment can also be organized to support emergent literacy learning. Design the schedule to ensure that there are opportunities throughout the day for children to engage in literacy activities with adults, peers, and alone. Examples of social arrangements include, but are not limited to, large group and small group teacher-led activities (e.g., story time, retelling stories, playing rhyme games, making books); one-to-one interactions with adults around books and other literacy materials and activities (e.g., reading a book together, dictating to the teacher); opportunities to engage with peers around literacy (e.g., looking at books together, writing a letter, taking orders at a pretend restaurant, making signs for the classroom, making waiting lists for favorite toys or activities, making up stories, acting out stories); as well as opportunities to independently engage with literacy materials such as books and writing materials.

Using Planned Activities and Teaching Strategies

As one plans routines and activities to support emergent literacy, focus on addressing emergent literacy outcomes in at least three areas: (1) comprehension, narrative, and vocabulary during book reading; (2) phonological awareness (i.e., sounds in language) and alphabetic principals; and (3) print concepts (Hanline, 2001; Neuman & Roskos, 1992). Table 2 summarizes three sets of teaching strategies that teachers can use to support children's learning in each of these three areas. Both the child outcomes and the teaching strategies listed are based on empirical research (e.g., National Reading Panel, 2000). However, it is important to note that we have organized the teaching skills in this way in order to highlight how different sets of skills relate logically to different aspects of emergent literacy, as well as to provide a way of thinking about how such strategies can be integrated into current practices.

In reality, there is much crossover in what children learn and in the strategies that foster this learning. For example, reading a book with children automatically includes skills from both Skill Sets 1 and 3. It also is important to remember that the lists in Table 2 do not cover all of the important areas of emergent literacy. For example, they do not address the development of basic knowledge, which also is important to later reading and writing (Neuman, Copple, & Bredekamp, 2000). Instead, we have chosen to focus on those skills that may be new to teachers as they seek to integrate emergent literacy learning into their current classroom curriculum and to emphasize these skills in relation to their most closely related child outcomes.

Embedding Strategies From the Skill Sets

When teachers are first learning to use the strategies listed in Table 2, it is often easiest to focus on and practice these skills during activities that they have planned specifically with the skills in mind. In this way, teachers increase the number of opportunities they have to practice the skills. However, we also know that it is important for children to have opportunities to engage in literacy activities across the day and teachers can plan opportunities throughout the day as well as respond to unplanned "teachable moments" related to emergent literacy. The following four vignettes, three of which focus on one of each of the skill sets and one that puts them all together, demonstrate how the teaching strategies might be implemented both during planned activities and in typical routines throughout the day.

> *it is important for children to have opportunities to engage in literacy activities across the day and teachers can plan opportunities throughout the day as well as respond to unplanned "teachable moments" related to emergent literacy.*

Learning From and About Books (Skill Set 1)

In Ms. Fern's room, the children are studying "how I express my feelings and emotions." Ms. Fern is reading the book On Monday When It Rained *(Kachenmeister, 1989). In this book, a young boy describes*

Table 2
Emergent Literacy Teaching Strategies and Related Child Outcomes

Skill Set 1: Comprehension, narrative, and vocabulary during book reading	
Teaching Strategies	**Related Child Outcomes**
• Introduce content of book • Talk about physical features of book • Sustain interest • Ask questions to promote thinking • Make comments that expand children's information • Involve children in reviewing/closing the story/book • Relate story to play centers or future activities or experiences	• Enjoyment of books and reading • Book handling knowledge • Comprehension of main ideas and story lines • Expansion of knowledge and vocabulary • Story structure as narrative • Purpose of nonstory books and print • Link to life experiences (books inform life, books are about life)
Skill Set 2: Phonological awareness (sounds in language), alphabetic principles	
• Emphasize characteristics of sounds and letters within age appropriate activities • Demonstrate and emphasize characteristics of sounds and words • Ask children to identify characteristics of sounds and words (with model or choice) • Ask children to demonstrate characteristics of sounds and words	• Have fun with and develop curiosity about sounds and words • Understand that words are made up of different sounds • Understand that sounds can be put together to make words • Understand that sounds occur at different places in words (beginning, middle, end) • Understand that words can be categorized based on beginning or ending sound • Understand that letters represent sounds • Beginning recognition of letters
Skill Set 3: Print concepts	
• Use print to represent ideas in a way that is obvious to children • Point out relationship between picture/object and associated print • Encourage use of writing in play • Point out print conventions • Model and explain how to use writing tools • Use words related to writing/reading	• Understand relationship between print and meaning • Enjoyment of writing • Understand that writing conveys ideas • Understand that writing can be used for different purposes • Understand basic concepts about writing (left/right, top/bottom) • Use of writing tools

something that happens to him each day and the way the event made him feel. Ms. Fern introduces the book at the beginning of circle time by reminding the children how it relates to their ongoing study of expressing feelings and emotions. Before reading the book, Ms. Fern asks the children to remember all the emotions they have talked about and she writes them on a chart at the front of the room. They list words such as "mad," "sad," "angry," "excited," "happy," and "embarrassed." She asks them to look at the front of the book and to guess what emotion the boy pictured on the cover might be feeling. The children guess different feelings, and Ms. Fern writes these on the chart paper. She then suggests that they look for the expression in the book to see if they guessed the correct feeling.

After discussing the author and illustrator, Ms. Fern asks the children where she should begin reading the book. As she reads each page about events that happened to the boy, she asks the children to guess how that made the boy feel. Ms. Fern has also developed a picture board with different feeling pictures and words. For children who have limited language abilities, she shows them the picture board, reads the names of the feelings and points to the faces as she reads them, and asks the children to point to the feeling they think describes the child in the book. She then turns the page, reads the feeling word, and has all the children make the facial expression associated with that word.

When Ms. Fern comes to the word "disappointed," one of the children says, "We didn't write that word on our paper." Ms. Fern writes it down and then asks the children to think of a time when they have felt disappointed. They read a few more pages and come to the word "proud." Ms. Fern asks the children to think of some things that they could do in the classroom to feel proud. The children are all very engaged in the book. As Ms. Fern reads each emotion, she alters her voice tone and makes facial expressions associated with the emotion she is reading. After reading a page, she says, "That made the little boy feel ... " and pauses to let the children guess the feeling. She also has small hand mirrors for the children so that they can look in a mirror as they make faces associated with the feeling words. Ms. Fern wants the children to begin to notice the emotions of other children in the classroom.

Once she has finished reading the book, Ms. Fern explains to the children that they are going to create a similar book about their own feelings during center time. Before each child leaves the group, Ms. Fern asks them to tell her what emotion from the book they want to include in their classroom book. The children are very excited. As a matter of fact, as Kai is leaving circle, he says, "I like the word excited.

I'm going to draw a picture about how excited I am when my granny comes to pick me up from school." When it is Jesse's turn to leave circle, Ms. Fern asks her for a word to include in the book. Jesse cannot remember any of the words and sits there with her head down. Ms. Fern walks over and says, "Jesse, look through the book and show me a picture you like." Jesse opens the book and finds a picture of the boy looking very happy. Ms. Fern tells her the feeling word and Jesse says that is the word she wants to include in the classroom book.

In this vignette, Ms. Fern uses many of the strategies from Skill Set 1. She introduces the content of the book by describing the book and connecting it to the unit the class is currently studying. She reviews vocabulary words in the book and relates them to words they have been studying. She also asks the children to predict how the boy is feeling based on his facial expression. She talks about the author and illustrator and then asks the children where she should begin reading as a strategy for reinforcing the children's understanding of the physical aspects of books. Ms. Fern sustains the children's interest in a number of ways including: altering her voice to match the child's feeling in the book, making faces, letting the children make faces in a mirror, and pausing to let the children guess what is coming on the following page. She asks a variety of questions that promote children's thinking and problem solving, such as asking the children what makes them feel certain ways, asking them to predict how the boy is feeling, and asking them to remember how certain things made them feel. She expands the children's information by talking about the meaning of the feeling words, relating the book to their previous discussion of feelings and emotions, and pointing out the relationship between different events and how they make one feel. Finally, Ms. Fern includes the children in reviewing the story by asking them to pick a word from the book that they want to include in their classroom book.

It is also important to note that Ms. Fern individualizes her instruction throughout this activity. For example, she has a picture board for children with limited language. At the end of the activity, when a child cannot remember a word, she looks through the book with the child and provides her with additional prompts to help her select a feeling word for their classroom book. It is also important to note how this activity combines opportunities for children to learn emergent literacy skills while also promoting children's social emotional development.

Awareness of Sounds in Words (Skill Set 2)

The children in Ms. Oster's classroom have become very interested in sounds and letters. Ms. Oster decides to begin focusing on rhym-

ing words. Some of the children are already beginning to use rhymes spontaneously, while other children don't yet seem aware of them. She introduces the concept of rhyming with a book that includes many rhyming words. During group time, she introduces the concept and reads the book. Each time there are rhyming words, she writes the rhyming words on a chart in front of the group. After she has read the book, she reviews the pairs of rhyming words together with the children, and then they generate additional examples of words that rhyme with each pair. For example, one of the sets of rhyming words in the story is "cat" and "bat." She asks the children to think of other rhyming words. Felicia, Debbie, Hasan, and Rahi begin saying words like "tat," "pat," "sat," and "rat."

Ms. Oster realizes that this task is too difficult for two of the children, Sammie and Omeed, so she turns to them and asks, "Hmmmm, does 'cat' rhyme with 'mat' or does 'cat' rhyme with 'dog'?" Omeed and Sammie are both able to choose the rhyming word. Ms. Oster also models rhyming words for two other children who are not able to make that choice by saying, "Riley and Sidney, I hear some words that sound alike ... 'cat,' 'mat,' 'sat,' and 'pat,'" giving them the opportunity to hear more examples of rhyming words. They end circle time by thinking of a word that rhymes with each of their names. This is hard for many of the children, so Ms. Oster pairs them up to leave circle and asks them to help each other think of a word that rhymes with their names.

As the children are leaving circle, she tells them that their teaching assistant, Mr. Jake, will be in the circle area to continue talking about rhyming words if any children are interested in choosing to do that. Omeed and Rahi choose to stay at the circle to play with Mr. Jake. He asks them to think of a rhyming word by naming their favorite animal, toy, or vehicle. Omeed says, "I saw a cow the other day." Before Mr. Jake can say anything, Rahi says, "I know, I know, 'cow' rhymes with 'wow'!" Mr. Jake responds, "And Omeed, does 'hat' rhyme with 'cow' or does 'how' rhyme with 'cow'?" Omeed answers, "Mr. Jake, you are silly—'hat' doesn't rhyme with cow, 'how' rhymes with 'cow'." As they name more rhyming words, Mr. Jake writes them on paper. When the boys say they are finished, Mr. Jake reads them the words and asks them to tell him what they did with the words. Mr. Jake writes down their answers and puts the papers in their cubbies so they can take them home and tell their parents about the rhyming activity.

In this vignette, Ms. Oster responds to the children's interest in rhyming by developing an activity that increases their understanding of how rhyming works. Both she and Mr. Jake use strategies from Skill Set 2. They use age-appropriate activities (e.g., book, child-selected game, use of children's own names) to promote children's understanding of sounds and the relationship between sounds and letters. Both teachers also seek to meet the needs of children with diverse abilities by using a range of prompts and supports. For example, they support rhyming by: (1) demonstrating rhymes (e.g., reading from the book and repeating rhyming words that the children generate); (2) providing choices; and (3) asking the children to make up rhymes. They also pair more skilled with less skilled children. The vignette also demonstrates the use of both large group and small group activities that support the same concept. Finally, Mr. Jake sounds out words as he writes them down, emphasizing the relationship between sounds and letters. Notice that he also embeds concepts about print (Skill Set 3, described following) into the activity by making a list the children can take home to help share with their families about what they are learning.

Awareness of Print Concepts (Skill Set 3)

The children in Mr. Li's classroom decide to create a new dramatic play area. As part of another unit, the class takes a vote on their favorite food. The winner by far is pizza. Mr. Li asks the children where they get their pizza. They talk about grocery stores, pizza shops, and delivery people. One of the children suggests that they turn the dramatic play area into a pizza shop. Since not all the children have been to a pizza shop, Mr. Li plans a walk to the pizza shop up the street. Among other things, Mr. Li asks the children to pay attention to all the signs at the pizza shop so they will know what signs they need to put up in their shop. While they are at the pizza shop, the children notice that there are signs that indicate the following: the name of the store, the address of the store, the hours of the store, whether the store is open or closed, and the prices of the different pizzas.

For several days following their trip to the pizza store, Mr. Li uses small group time to get materials ready for their new dramatic play area. He plans a small group activity of making signs for their new shop. Mr. Li leads the activity with four children at a time. At the beginning of the activity, Mr. Li asks the children to remind him about what signs they need to make. As each child lists a sign, Mr. Li writes it down. Once they have generated the list, Mr. Li reads the list back while pointing to the words. The first group of children decides to make the sign that tells the hours of the store. Mr. Li asks the children what they need to make the sign and the children decide to use markers, glue and glitter, and paper. Mr. Li gets a variety of markers, including some that have a built-up grip for Jaymin, a child with cerebral palsy. They discuss what needs to be on the sign and decide on the following: "Store Hours, noon to midnight." The children take turns writing the letters. Some children can copy a model of the letter, others need verbal prompts (e.g., draw a circle), while others need physical assistance holding the marker and writing the letters. As they are writing the letters, Mr. Li talks to the children about the letters and words they are writing, the direction of the words, and the location of the letters in relation to each other. After they finish making the sign, Mr. Li reads the sign as he points to the words. One of the children then asks if she can read the sign. Toward the end of the activity, one of the children has an idea that there also needs to be a menu. That is a task on which the next small group can work.

In this vignette, Mr. Li plans a variety of opportunities for helping the children to learn about print. He uses many of the strategies in Skill Set 3. He begins by asking the children to notice all the signs at the pizza shop. This is important in terms of supporting children in learning about print in their everyday environments. Mr. Li writes down a list of signs as the children generate ideas. He reads the list back to them as a way of connecting their ideas with the printed word. He gives them choices about writing utensils and provides assistance when needed, making specific adaptations for children with special needs. He points out print conventions by talking about where the letters go, where to begin writing, and the direction of the writing. He talks to them about words related to print, including "letters" and "words."

Putting it All Together

Each of the three previous vignettes describes a scenario in which the teacher focuses on a specific skill set primarily in planned activities. The following vignette expands this information by showing how all of the skill sets can be integrated across the day.

Mr. Bishop's preschool classroom is taking a field trip to the fire station. This is an annual event that typically coincides with fire safety week. This year, Mr. Bishop is working hard to embed emergent literacy instruction across the day, including days when they go on field trips. Mr. Bishop plans several activities related to the field trip that he will use to support the children's early literacy development. First, he selects a book about fire safety and fire stations. He reads this book during group time for several days before the field trip. Before reading the book, he reminds the children that they will be going to a fire station. As they read the book, they talk about things that they will see and learn at the fire station. He asks the children to predict how the fire station will be the same as or different than the fire station in the book. He also asks the children to think of questions that they might want to ask the firefighters. As they generate questions, he writes them on a chart paper. They generate questions like, "Do you sleep at the fire station?", "Do you have a dog at the fire station?", and "Are you scared when you go to a fire?"

Second, Mr. Bishop devises a game that the children can play while waiting in line to get on and off the bus and while riding the bus. He will say a word, and then he will ask each child to think of a word that begins with the same sound. He starts off by saying "bus." Jesse says "baby," Hillary says "bat," and Jose says "beast." He looks at Andre, who can't think of a word. Mr. Bishop gives Andre two words to choose from: "Andre, does 'bat' start with the same sound as 'bus,' or does 'cat' start with the same sound as 'bus'? Listen while I say them together: 'bat/bus' or 'cat/bus'?" After all the children have had a turn, Mr. Bishop calls on a child to pick a new word. This game continues throughout the bus ride to the fire station.

Another activity that Mr. Bishop uses to promote literacy while on the field trip is related to teaching the children about print in their environment. Once they are at the fire station, and after they have heard from the firefighters, Mr. Bishop asks the children to look around the fire station and the fire truck for all the print they can find. At first, the children point out the obvious print. For example, they find the name of the fire station on the door, the print on the side of the fire truck, and the names of the firefighters on their badges. As the station tour continues, however, the children find print in even the most obscure places. There is print on the tires, the window of the fire truck, the signs to the bathroom, the letters on the phone, and the vending machines ... in fact, there is print everywhere! As the children get on the bus, they find even more print on the side of the bus, on the dashboard, on the road signs. Mr. Bishop and the parents who are volunteering on the field trip begin talking with the children about all the other places they see print. The children talk about papers, magazines, TV commercials, menus at restaurants, signs on the road, signs in stores, and many other locations.

The following day, the children begin developing a book about their trip to the fire station. As a large group, they retell the events of the trip as the teaching assistant writes their words on a chart. During small group, the children tell the teachers about their favorite part of the trip, the teachers write the information down, and the children draw a picture related to their favorite part of the trip.

This vignette demonstrates many aspects of using the three sets of teaching strategies. First, the vignette shows the range of possible contexts for supporting children's emergent literacy development. Mr. Bishop supports children's emergent literacy development during story time, while riding the bus, during transitions, during the visit to the fire station, and during small and large group activities. Second, it demonstrates the extent to which the skills are interrelated. For example, during the large group, the children are asked to recall facts about their trip (Skill Set 1), which are then written down on the chart paper (Skill Set 3). Third, the vignette demonstrates how Mr. Bishop adapts his teaching strategies to meet the needs of individual children. When one of the children is not able to think of a word that begins with the "b" sound, he gives the child some choices. Finally, this vignette demonstrates how strategies for supporting children's emergent literacy can be embedded into an ongoing curriculum.

Some ideas for using the teaching strategies to address multiple emergent literacy skills during classroom routines are included in the embedding matrix shown in Table 3. For example, children can clap

Table 3
Matrix of Skills Embedded in Routine Activities in the Classroom

Activity	Comprehension, Narrative, and Vocabulary	Phonological Awareness, Alphabetic Principles	Print Concepts
Arrival and/or Departure	As children enter the room, tell them about the "word of the day" and what it means. As they leave, ask them to tell about the "word of the day."	Tell children to line up to go to the bus when the teacher says the sound with which their name begins. Have children find a friend to go to the buses with whose name begins with the same sound as their name.	Children sign in with their name. *(Adaptations that might be needed include writing utensils with built-up grasps for children who have motor problems, samples of the children's names for those children who cannot yet write their name, adult assistance for those who cannot write their name.)* As children leave, ask, "What was your favorite thing you did today?" Write each response on a chart with the child and discuss at group the following day.

Table 3 (*continued*)

Activity	Comprehension, Narrative, and Vocabulary	Phonological Awareness, Alphabetic Principles	Print Concepts
Snack	Start a story and have children take turns adding a line to the story.	Play "I Spy": Have children look for objects that begin with a certain sound or that rhyme with a certain word. Have children think of food words that begin with a certain sound.	Have children make a menu for snack and then have children read it or point to what they are having. The menu could include both pictures and words. Tape name cards on the table and talk about the letters or sounds in children's names while they are eating.
Transitions	As children wait, remind them of the book that was read during story time and ask them about their favorite part. Give each child a card with a word and a picture. Have them identify the word and make up a sentence about their word.	Put small objects in a brown bag. As children are waiting for others, pull out an object and have children think of a word that rhymes with the object, or starts or ends with the same sound. Have children clap or match the number of syllables in their name as they go from circle to centers.	As children move through the hallway, encourage them to find things that have print on them. During circle, have children list all the things they saw with print when they were walking down the hall. Children can help make a sign that shows the steps of cleaning up after center. The teacher can write what the children say and the children can draw pictures to go along with the steps.

the number of syllables in the "Daily Magic Word" as they transition to their turn to wash hands for snack or as they enter a play area. Or name cards taped on the snack table can be used to reinforce left to right reading and finding whose names have the same letters. Beginning sounds also can be emphasized in any of these situations, as can rhymes, by just playing games to think about more words that "start the same" or "sound the same." Not only are these teaching opportunities useful for promoting learning, they can also be a very motivating way to keep children engaged in learning throughout the day. While it won't be possible to do everything on the matrix every day, the matrix provides a tool for generating ideas for embedding emergent literacy skills into routine activities across the day. It is also possible to expand the matrix to include other activities during the day (e.g., centers, small group, large group).

Ensuring that the teaching strategies are adapted for the abilities and needs of all the children requires careful planning. For example, when reading books, teachers can think of questions ahead of time, write them on sticky notes, and put them in the book. The matrix included in Table 3 could be used to plan for modifications and adaptations for individual children as well. Teachers can think about each of the activities they include in the matrix and consider what adaptations would be needed for the children in the classroom. (In Table 3, an example adaptation is shown in italics in the matrix under Print Concepts.)

Ensuring that the teaching strategies are adapted for the abilities and needs of all the children requires careful planning.

Conclusion

Spending time on emergent literacy can be a great deal of fun for both teachers and children. Children are interested and highly motivated when teachers take the time to use these teaching skills, and quickly reward teachers with plenty of evidence of their learning. However, it requires careful planning on the part of the teacher to ensure that activities are highly engaging *and* address the needs of all children.

Spending time on emergent literacy can be a great deal of fun for both teachers and children.

Notes

Preparation of this manuscript was supported by a field-initiated research grant, "The Effects of Individual and Group Interventions on Emerging Literacy Skills in Young Children" (Office of Special Education Programs, U.S. Department of Education, #H324C030114A).

You can reach Mary Louise Hemmeter by e-mail at mlhemm@uiuc.edu

References

Bowman, B. T., Donovan, M. S., & Burns, M. S. (Eds.). (2001). *Eager to learn: Educating our preschoolers*. (Report, National Research Council, Committee on Early Childhood Pedagogy.) Washington, DC: National Academy Press.

Burns, S., Griffin, P., & Snow, C. (1999). *Starting out right: A guide to promoting children's reading success*. Washington, DC: National Academy Press.

Hanline, M. F. (2001). Supporting emergent literacy in play-based activities. *Young Exceptional Children, 4*(4), 10–15.

IDEA. (1997). Individuals with Disabilities Education Act Amendments of 1997, 20, U.S.C., §140.

International Reading Association (IRA)/National Association for the Education of Young Children (NAEYC). (1998, May). *Overview of learning to read and write: Developmentally appropriate practices for young children. Position statement*. Washington, DC: Author.

Kachenmeister, C. (1989). *On Monday when it rained*. Boston: Houghton Mifflin.

Light, J., & Kelford-Smith, A. K. (1993). Home literacy experiences of preschoolers who use AAC systems and of their nondisabled peers. *Augmentative and Alternative Communication, 9*, 10–25.

Lyon, G. R. (2002, April). *A summit on early childhood cognitive development: Summary comments*. Washington, DC: U.S. Department of Education. Retrieved June 30, 2005, from http://www.ed.gov/offices/OESE/earlychildhood/summit/lyon.html.

Marvin, C. (1995). Home literacy experiences of preschool children with single and multiple disabilities. *Topics in Early Childhood Special Education, 14*, 436–454.

Marvin, C. A., & Wright, D. (1997). Literacy socialization in the homes of preschool children. *Language, Speech, & Hearing Services in the Schools, 28*, 154–163.

National Reading Panel. (2000). *Report of the National Reading Panel. Teaching children to read: An evidence-based assessment of the scientific research literature on reading and its implications for reading instruction* (NIH Publication No. 00–4769). Washington, DC: U.S. Government Printing Office. Retrieved June 30, 2005, from http://www.nichd.nih.gov/publications/nrp/smallbook.htm.

Neuman, S. B., Copple, C., & Bredekamp, S. (2000). *Learning to read and write: Developmentally appropriate practices for young children*. Washington, DC: National Association for the Education of Young Children (NAEYC).

Neuman, S. B., & Roskos, K. (1992). Literacy objects as cultural tools: Effects on children's literacy behaviors in play. *Reading Research Quarterly, 27*, 203–225.

Notari-Syverson, A., O'Connor, R. E., & Vadasy, P. F. (1998). *Ladders to literacy: A preschool activity book*. Baltimore: Paul H. Brookes.

Snow, C. E., Burns, S., & Griffin, P. (Eds.). (1998). *Preventing reading difficulties in young children*. (Committee on Learning Research and Practice, National Research Council.) Washington, DC: National Academy Press.

U.S. Department of Education (USDOE). (2001). *Put reading first: The research building blocks for teaching children to read*. Washington, DC: Author.

Whitehurst, G. J., & Lonigan, C. J. (2001). Emergent literacy: Development from prereaders to readers. In S. Neuman & D. Dickinson (Eds.), *Handbook of early literacy development* (pp. 11–29). New York: Guilford.

Using Storybooks With Preschool Children:

Enhancing Language and Emergent Literacy

Rebecca B. McCathren, Ph.D.,
University of Missouri

Jill Howard Allor, Ed.D.,
Southern Methodist University, Dallas, TX

Using storybooks effectively is important in preparing preschoolers for reading acquisition. Typically, reading problems begin very early in a child's education and often persist and negatively impact his or her ability to participate in jobs or daily life skills as adults (Stanovich, 1993/1994). In order to prevent reading problems, preschool children must be as prepared as possible to learn to read. The importance of preparing children to learn to read cannot be overemphasized. This preparation should include general language development, as well as basic insights into phonology and its relationship to print (Snow, Burns, & Griffin, 1998; Sulzby & Teale, 1991). These are all critical elements of emergent literacy.

Using storybooks in the preschool classroom has long been recognized as important and is generally a common practice. Research demonstrates that interactive storybook reading produces substantial gains in the oral language development of preschoolers, particularly those who have language delays (Bus, van Ijzendoorn, & Pelligrini, 1995; Dale, Crain-Thoreson, Notari-Syverson, & Cole, 1996; Karweit, 1989; Mautte, 1990; Valdez-Menchaca & Whitehurst, 1992). In addition to fostering language development, storybook reading with preschool children has been correlated to a variety of reading factors, including children's eagerness to read, becoming literate before formal schooling, and success in beginning reading programs in elementary school (see Sulzby & Teale, 1991). Currently, researchers are learning more about how to use storybooks as an effective means of fostering language and literacy development in young children (see Bus, Ijzendoorn, & Pellegrini, 1995; Scarborough & Dobrich, 1994 for reviews). In general, rather than reading the book word for word adults should use interactive strategies to facilitate the development of both receptive and expressive language skills (Arnold & Whitehurst, 1994; Mautte, 1990). These strategies are most effective when done with one or two children at a time, making parents ideal implementers.

It is imperative that preschool children, especially those considered at risk, participate in activities and interactions that facilitate the early development of literacy. In other words, preschoolers need to interact with the meaning, sounds, and print of our language (International Reading Association [IRA] & National Association for the Education of Young Children [NAEYC], 1998). This can be achieved by engaging children in storybook reading activities. The purpose of this article is to help teachers and parents develop a range of strategies for using storybooks to help facilitate language and literacy in young children. In any preschool classroom, there may be children who are just beginning to label pictures (including children with language disabilities and children learning English as their second language) as well as children who are beginning to pay attention to words and print. Teachers must be well-equipped to meet the diverse needs of these children. In this article, we: (1) provide an overview of the critical elements of emergent literacy, (2) discuss specific strategies for using storybooks with preschoolers to facilitate language development and emergent literacy skills, and (3) provide specific strategies for children learning English as a second language.

Critical Elements of Emergent Literacy

Oral Language: Vocabulary and Narrative Skills

Oral vocabulary and narrative skills are critical to the development of emergent literacy. As a language-based skill, reading shares many of the processes and knowledge involved in using and understanding language for social conversation (Kamhi & Catts, 1999). Young children who have disabilities or delays in the development of language are at higher risk for reading disabilities (Snow et al., 1998). School-age children experiencing difficulties in reading often also have difficulty with the development of expressive and receptive vocabulary and narrative skills, i.e., the ability to tell or understand a story. Early vocabulary development also is important because it has been positively correlated with children's reading ability in the primary grades (Walker, Greenwood, Hart, & Carta, 1994). Many children, particularly those from low-income families, arrive at school with poorly developed vocabularies (Hart & Risley, 1995; Rush, 1999), thus making it more difficult to learn to read.

Oral Language: Phonological Awareness

Oral language development includes the ability to understand sounds, words, and phrases for the purpose of communicating ideas. Phonological awareness is the understanding that oral language is composed of sounds or groups of sounds, and is an important emergent literacy skill because it has been demonstrated to help young children learn to read (Byrne & Fielding-Barnsley, 1993; O'Connor, Jenkins, Leicester, & Slocum, 1993). Identifying beginning sounds in spoken words and recognizing that two words rhyme are examples of phonological awareness. Phonological awareness training results in improved phonological awareness, more rapid response to beginning reading instruction, and improved reading development (Byrne & Fielding-Barnsley, 1993; O'Connor et al., 1993).

Print Awareness

In addition to oral language, young children need an appreciation of print as communicative. Storybooks can be used to help children attend to the forms and functions of written language. In order to learn to read, young children must develop basic insights and observations about print (Adams, 1990). As Durkin (1993) explains, these insights are gained through meaningful experiences with text. Young children must: (1) know the difference between graphic displays of words and nonwords; (2) know that print corresponds to speech, word by word; (3) understand the function of empty space in establishing word boundaries; and (4) understand that we read English from left to right and top to bottom (Durkin, 1993). Letter recognition can also be included as a form of print awareness (Adams, 1990). Some educators have debated the necessity of teaching young children the names of letters, but it is clear that children must learn how to readily recognize and discriminate the visual shapes of letters before they will be able to learn to read (Adams, 1990). Although children may become familiar with letters in a variety of ways (e.g., blocks and magnetic letters), it is critical that they attend to letters and their sounds in print (Lesiak, 1997).

Strategies for Using Storybooks

A variety of storybooks may be used for preparing young children to read. Those appropriate for preschoolers should contain interesting pictures, predictable language, rhymes, and repetitive initial sounds. Although many preschool children are not ready to participate in formal reading instruction, some children are very eager to learn to read.

Adults can provide instruction that is responsive to this desire and is still developmentally appropriate (Bredekamp & Copple, 1997; IRA & NAEYC, 1998). The key to providing appropriate activities is recognizing the various abilities of preschool children. Teachers and parents should use short, playful activities to meet the varying needs and interest levels of the children. Following is a description of strategies for using storybooks to facilitate language development and emergent literacy in preschool children. The strategies do not have to be used in any specific order, although Storybook Preview should be used when a new book is introduced.

> *Teachers and parents should use short, playful activities to meet the varying needs and interest levels of the children.*

Storybook Preview

It is important to conduct Storybook Preview with very small groups of children or individual children in order to allow teachers to interact effectively with the children, responding to and expanding upon each child's communicative initiation. In Storybook Preview, the child explores the content of the book by labeling or talking about the pictures without regard to storyline. To build vocabulary, the adult may provide labels for the objects, actions, or events in which the child shows interest. For children in the early stages of language development, including children learning English as a second language, the adult can model one- or two-word phrases related to the pictures and expand the child's labels. For example, if the child points to a picture and says "doggie," the adult expands the label to more fully describe the picture (e.g., "doggie runs").

Many preschool classrooms may have children who are not able to label pictures because they do not yet produce speech; they are unable to make the connection among the word, the picture, and its "real life" referent; or they do not yet speak English. Adults can supply objects for children to hold and manipulate while pointing out the connection between the picture and its real life referent. Both children and adults can act out the actions in a story to facilitate the connection among the word, the picture, and the experience. This "acting out" strategy can be done for the story as a whole with children either providing the words and actions or just acting as the adult reads. Alternatively, the child can demonstrate discrete actions related to the story. For example, "The boy jumped way up. Let's see you jump. Right, jump, jump, jump. See, the boy jumped."

For children with more developed oral language, the adult should respond to questions and comments. When looking at a book during Storybook Preview a child may initiate a statement linking the book content to his or her life. For example, "We have a dog at home." The adult then has the opportunity to ask questions about the child's dog and to help the child identify likenesses and differences with the dog in the book, or to have the child engage in narrative activities about his or her dog that relate to the content and pictures in the story. The adult may repeat general questions as the child labels objects and actions in the pictures, such as, "What do you think is happening here?" In addition, the adult can ask questions that will prompt language but also help children to attend to other features of the pictures, such as "Look at her face; how do you think she's feeling?" or "Why do you think his eyes are closed?"

When looking at a book during Storybook Preview a child may initiate a statement linking the book content to his or her life.

Cole and Maddox (1997) have developed a video training tape for parents about how to use books with young children. Parents or caregivers are instructed that their role in the book reading activity is to be the bridge between the book and the child's learning. Books can be used to help children learn that pictures stand for real things just like printed words, to say and understand new words, and better ways of saying what they want to say. Parents are cautioned to talk about the pictures instead of reading all the words. The strategies suggested have an acronym CAR, which stands for Comment, Ask, and Respond.

Storybook Read Aloud

Reading aloud with young children can target the development of concepts of print, as well as language. In a large group, the teacher can read the book in a way that is designed to hold the attention of all the children. Choosing books with repetitive phrases or rhyming words can be effective for the development of literacy skills as well as make it easy to engage children. Pausing to allow children to fill in the repetitive phrases and rhyming words can also help keep their attention. In addition, having props related to the story may facilitate comprehension as well as help children stay focused. As a follow-up, an adult can read the story to smaller groups of children or an individual child, pointing to each word as it is being read. In order for this strategy to be effective, the children must all be sitting close enough to clearly see the print and must already have basic language skills. An adult can help each child choose his or her favorite page in the book for the adult to read again more slowly, pointing to only one word at a time. The child can talk about how the picture on a particular page relates to the words. Then the child can point to individual words for the adult to read. These additional activities will be important to develop a clear understanding of the words on the page and the purpose of spacing between words. It is not essential that an entire story be read in each sitting. The adult may wish to pull out a favorite book and read only certain parts of the story (e.g., the ending), or the child's favorite parts, when focusing on these print features.

Storybook Sounds

Storybook Sounds focuses on the development of phonological awareness using words and ideas from specific storybooks. These activities include identifying rhyming words and initial sounds. They should supplement a more complete plan to develop phonological awareness. Resources for phonological awareness activities and curricula are now widely available (e.g., *Ladders to Literacy* [Notari-Syverson, O'Connor, & Vadasy, 1998]; *Phonemic Awareness in Young Children* [Adams, Foorman, Lundberg, & Beeler, 1998]; and *Road to the Code* [Blachman, Ball, Black, & Tangel, 2000]). Storybook Sounds activities are patterned after these types of instructional programs. Yet they are different from general phonological awareness activities because they use words or

As with all activities for pre-schoolers, adults should capitalize on children's interests and skills as much as possible, and it is critical that adults know which words in books are appropriate for phonological awareness activities.

ideas directly taken from or related to familiar storybooks. As with all activities for preschoolers, adults should capitalize on children's interests and skills as much as possible, and it is critical that adults know which words in books are appropriate for phonological awareness activities. The difficulty of the activities and the words chosen for activities should be carefully tailored to the individual needs of preschoolers.

Generally, phonological awareness develops in phases. First, young children recognize that spoken sentences are made up of words. Then they begin to understand that words are made up of syllables. Finally, they become sensitive to individual sounds (phonemes) within words and are able to manipulate those sounds. This level of phonological awareness is often referred to by a more specific term, phoneme (or phonemic) awareness. Two main skills at this level are segmenting and blending. Segmenting tasks require children to isolate individual sounds in words, whereas blending tasks require children to put sounds together to form words. However, either of these tasks is appropriate for preschool children who have mastered awareness of words and rhyming sounds.

Three other points are critical in providing developmentally appropriate phonological awareness activities. First, phonological awareness is not a skill that can be clearly explained to young children. Instead of describing what to do, adults should model for the children and reinforce attempts to mimic the model. Children should never be allowed to become frustrated in their efforts to identify a rhyming word or repeat a series of sounds related to a story. All activities should include some responses that are simple enough for all or at least most children to answer correctly. For example, if an adult chooses to engage a child in an activity to develop syllable awareness, he or she would need to choose some very simple one- and two-syllable words along with more challenging words. For instance, if a child expresses interest in the crocodile in Eric Carle's (1997) *From Head to Toe*, the adult could ask the child to say the parts of the word and clap once for each part (syllable), modeling as needed. He or she would also want to choose simpler words such as cat or donkey. Although some children may be able to correctly clap for each syllable, other children may only begin to realize that some words are longer than others. Additionally, if a child does not respond quickly (usually within three to four seconds), the adult should simply model an acceptable response. Repeated exposure to these concepts is critical to phonological awareness development, particularly for children with disabilities. Additional thinking time may be necessary for some children with particularly slow processing rates.

Second, surprisingly, pronouncing phonemes in isolation is not always simple. Adults might enlist the help of speech therapists as they practice pronouncing sounds in isolation. Adults need to be sure that they are pronouncing sounds clearly and as they are pronounced in words. For example, the "f" in fan is pronounced /f/, not /fuh/. It is even better to stretch the sound, /fff/. Additionally, there is no need to associate every sound with a letter name. For preschool children, a focus on a limited number of sounds in familiar words is sufficient.

Third, adults must select words for activities that have simple linguistic structures. Phonological awareness tasks are simpler if words have fewer phonemes and do not begin with initial consonant clusters (Treiman & Weatherston, 1992). Because these activities are oral, adults may choose words with more complicated spellings as long as they contain only a few phonemes. For example, "may" and "eight" both have only two phonemes (/ma/ and /at/) and would be appropriate for use in oral phonological awareness activities with preschoolers. It also is easier to blend and segment words with initial phonemes that are continuous. Phonemes such as /s/ or /f/ can be "stretched," making words beginning with these phonemes easier to blend than those beginning with stop sounds, such as /b/ or /d/. See Table 1 for additional sample activities.

Storybook Celebration

In Storybook Celebration, children respond to the storybook through a motivating activity related to the meaning of the book. These activities

Table 1
Sample Phonological Awareness Activities

Sample activities with the storybook _Bread, Bread, Bread_ (Morris, 1989):

Child: My favorite page is the one with the woman cooking in the fire.

Simple Syllable Awareness Activity

Adult response: Let's say the parts of the word "cooking" while we clap.

Adult and child/ren: Cook-ing (clapping twice)

Adult: Now let's do the same thing with "fire."

Adult and child/ren: Fire (clapping once)

Adult: Which word is longer? Cook-ing (claps twice) or fire (claps once)?

Child/ren: Cooking.

Adult: Right. Cook-ing has two parts and fire only has one.

Identifying Initial Phoneme (Early Segmenting Task)

Adult response: I'm going to read that page again. This time I want you to listen for a word that begins with the /fff/ sound. What sound are you listening for?

Child/ren: /fff/.

Adult: Right. Listen for a word beginning with /fff/. (Adult reads text "cooking bread over the fire," stretching the /fff/ in fire if the children need a hint.) Which word did I read that began with /fff/?

Child/ren: Fire.

Blending Onset and Rime

Adult response: I have a mystery word for that page. See if you can guess my word. Listen to the sounds: /fff/ /ire/. What's the word?

Child/ren: Fire.

(If necessary, the adult can have the child/ren say different words related to the picture and ask each time, "Is that /fff/ /ire/?" If the child/ren have difficulty the adult should be careful not to pause between the onset and the rime, /fffire/.)

---

can be used with children who are just beginning to label pictures as well as those who are able to participate in more advanced literacy activities. Follow-up art, cooking, science, or other activities can extend learning and help children bridge what is in books to other parts of their lives. For example, *Bread, Bread, Bread* (Morris, 1989) is a book of photographs of people of various cultures from around the world and the kinds of foods they use as "bread." Story Celebration could begin with a discussion of the kinds of bread the children in a particular classroom eat at home. The children also could make different kinds of bread with an adult and create their own recipes. In addition, the kinds of bread displayed in the book could be sampled by the children. The ways to celebrate storybooks are only limited by the imaginations of adults and the children. The only stipulations for activities are that they: (1) be motivating to young children, (2) relate to the meaning of the storybook, and (3) are meaningful to the children. Skillful adults will capitalize on children's past experiences as well as provide new experiences that relate to the stories they are reading.

> *In Storybook Celebration, children respond to the storybook through a motivating activity related to the meaning of the book.*

Children Learning English as a Second Language

According to the U. S. Census Bureau (1995), 15% of all children from five to 17 years of age in America live in families where English is not the primary language. For children enrolled in a Head Start program those numbers are even higher, with 26% speaking languages other than English (Head Start Bureau, 2000). In general, school experiences should support the continued development of the child's primary language while providing meaningful experiences with English (IRA, 1997). Strategies to support the development of the primary language while using storybooks include: (1) add the primary language translation to familiar stories, (2) send translated books home, (3) establish a lending library that includes books written in the children's primary language(s), and (4) have fluent speakers of the child's primary language (e.g., teachers, instructional assistants, parent volunteers, older children) read and engage the child in early literacy activities in the primary language (Espinosa & Burns, 2003). English language development can be facilitated using the language strategies discussed previously in this article. It is important to remember that children will not learn literacy skills in a language they do not yet speak (L. Espinosa, personal communication, December, 2001).

Summary

In conclusion, storybook reading should be used strategically in preschool classrooms to develop language and prepare preschoolers to learn to read. Teachers and parents should develop and capitalize upon young children's love of stories and pictures. It is essential that storybook activities engage children purposefully and actively in the meaning, phonology, and print of storybooks. When designed according to the individual abilities of preschoolers, these activities will foster the development of receptive and expressive vocabulary, narrative skills, phonological awareness, and print awareness. In this article we described specific strategies for developing these abilities in ways that are appropriate for preschool children. These types of activities should become part of the daily routines of preschool classrooms and preschool teachers should also encourage their use at home. Providing this foundation in preschool will increase future success in language and reading.

Note
You can reach Rebecca B. McCathren by e-mail at mccathrenr@missouri.edu

References
Adams, M. J. (1990). *Beginning to read: Thinking and learning about print.* Cambridge: MIT Press.
Adams, M. J., Foorman, B. R., Lundberg, I., & Beeler, T. (1998). *Phonemic awareness in young children.* Baltimore: Paul H. Brookes.
Arnold, D. S., & Whitehurst, G. J. (1994). Accelerating language development through picture book reading: A summary of dialogic reading and its effects. In D. K. Dickinson (Ed.), *Bridges to literacy: Children, families, and school* (pp. 103–128). Cambridge: Blackwell.
Blachman, B. A., Ball, E. W., Black, R., & Tangel, D. M. (2000). *Road to the code.* Baltimore: Paul H. Brookes.
Bredecamp, S., & Copple, C. (1997). *Developmentally appropriate practice in early childhood programs* (Rev. ed.). Washington, DC: National Association for the Education of Young Children (NAEYC).
Bus, A. G., van Ijzendoorn, M. H., & Pellegrini, A. D. (1995). Joint book reading makes for success in learning to read: A meta-analysis on intergenerational transmission of literacy. *Review of Educational Research, 65*(1), 1–21.
Byrne, B., & Fielding-Barnsley, R. (1993). Evaluation of a program to teach phonemic awareness to young children: One-year follow-up. *Journal of Educational Psychology, 85,* 104–111.
Carle, E. (1997). *From head to toe.* New York: HarperCollins Juvenile.
Cole, K., & Maddox, M. (1997). *Talking and books: Language is the key* [Video]. (Available from Kevin Cole, Ph.D., Washington Research Institute, 150 Nickerson Street, Suite 305, Seattle, WA 98109.)
Dale, P. S., Crain-Thoreson, C., Notari-Syversen, A., & Cole, K. (1996). Parent-child book reading as an intervention technique for young children with language delays. *Topics in Early Childhood Special Education, 16,* 13–35.
Durkin, D. (1993). *Teaching them to read.* Boston: Allyn & Bacon.
Espinosa, L. M., & Burns, M. S. (2003). Early literacy for young children and English language learners. In C. L. Howes (Ed.), *Teaching 4- to 8-year-olds: Literacy, math, multiculturalism, and classroom community* (pp. 88–114). Baltimore: Paul H. Brookes.
Hart, B., & Risley, T. R. (1995). *Meaningful differences in the everyday experience of young American children.* Baltimore: Paul H. Brookes.
Head Start Bureau. (2000). *Celebrating cultural diversity in Head Start.* Washington, DC: Commissioner's Office of Research and Evaluation and Head Start Bureau.

International Reading Association (IRA). (1997). *The role of phonics in reading instruction* (Position statement of IRA). Newark, DE: International Reading Association.

International Reading Association (IRA) and National Association for the Education of Young Children (NAEYC). (1998). *Learning to read and write: Developmentally appropriate practices for young children* (Joint position of the IRA and NAEYC). Newark, DE: International Reading Association.

Kamhi, A. G., & Catts, H. W. (1999). Language and reading: Convergence and divergence. In H. W. Catts & A. G. Kamhi (Eds.), *Language and reading disabilities* (pp. 1–24). Boston: Allyn & Bacon.

Karweit, N. (1989). The effects of a story-reading program on the vocabulary and story comprehension skills of disadvantaged preschool and kindergarten children. *Early Education and Development, 1,* 105–114.

Lesiak, J. L. (1997). Research-based answers to questions about emergent literacy in kindergarten. *Psychology in the Schools, 34,* 143–160.

Mautte, L. A. (1990). The effects of adult-interactive behaviors within the context of repeated storybook reading upon the language development and selected prereading skills of prekindergarten at-risk children. *Florida Education Research Council Research Bulletin, 22*(3), 1–31.

Morris, A. (1989). *Bread, bread, bread.* New York: Scholastic.

Notari-Syverson, A., O'Connor, R. E., & Vadasy, P. F. (1998). *Ladders to literacy.* Baltimore: Paul H. Brookes.

O'Connor, R. E., Jenkins, J. R., Leicester, N., & Slocum, T. A. (1993). Teaching phonological awareness to young children with learning disabilities. *Exceptional Children, 59,* 532–546.

Rush, K. L. (1999). Caregiver-child interactions and early literacy development of preschool children from low-income backgrounds. *Topics in Early Childhood Special Education, 19,* 3–14.

Scarborough, H. S., & Dobrich, W. (1994). Another look at parent-preschooler bookreading: How naked is the emperor? *Developmental Review, 14*(3), 340–347.

Snow, C. E., Burns, M. S., & Griffin, P. (1998). *Preventing reading difficulties in young children.* Washington, DC: National Academy Press.

Stanovich, K. E. (1993/1994). Romance and reality. *The Reading Teacher, 47,* 280–290.

Sulzby, E., & Teale, W. (1991). Emergent literacy. In R. Barr, M. L. Kamil, P. B. Mosenthal, & P. D. Pearson (Eds.), *Handbook of reading research: Volume II* (pp. 727–757). New York: Longman.

Treiman, R., & Weatherston, S. (1992). Effects of linguistic structure on children's ability to identify initial consonants. *Journal of Educational Psychology, 84,* 174–181.

U. S. Bureau of Census. (1995). *The Hispanic population in the U. S.* Washington, DC: Department of Commerce, U. S. Bureau of Census.

Valdez-Menchaca, M. C., & Whitehurst, G. J. (1992). Accelerating language development through picture book reading: A systematic extension to Mexican daycare. *Developmental Psychology, 28*(6), 1106–1114.

Walker, D., Greenwood, C., Hart, B., & Carta, J. (1994). Prediction of school outcomes based on language production and socioeconomic factors. *Child Development, 65,* 606–621.

Let's Give 'em Something to Talk About:

The Language Arts and Science Connection

Sallee J. Beneke, M.Ed.,
Michaelene M. Ostrosky, Ph.D., and
Lilian G. Katz, Ph.D.,
University of Illinois at Urbana-Champaign

A few four-year olds are sitting together under a tree on the playground. Nico stands and enthusiastically jumps up and down to show how his new shoes light up. Taylor and Dillon are also wearing sneakers that light up when they step down on them, and they begin to jump. Their teacher, Mrs. Amaya, notices their interest in this phenomenon and starts a discussion about the lights:

Mrs. Amaya: Wow! Look at your shoes! That is so cool. They light up when you step down.

Nico: Yup, they do. Watch this (jumps up and down several times).

Mrs. Amaya: How does that happen? How do they light up?

Nico: Because they are new.

Mrs. Amaya: Mine are new too, but they don't light up.

Taylor: No, because they light up when you step on them (steps down hard several times).

Mrs. Amaya: (Steps down hard several times) That's funny, mine don't light up when I step down.

Dillon: No, no, no, you have to have these holes (points to the holes).

Mrs. Amaya: (Pointing to holes in her own shoe) But I have holes, and mine still don't light up, and Josh has holes in his sneakers too, and his do not light up, either. I wonder why.

Emily: I think you need batteries. Yes, you need batteries.

Nico: Yeah, you need batteries to make them work. (Thinks for a while) But I did not see batteries when I put my toes in.

Emily: I think they are under the toes.

Taylor: I can't feel the batteries under my toes.

Mrs. Amaya: I wonder how we can find out about this?

In the vignette, Mrs. Amaya skillfully uses children's curiosity about a scientific phenomenon to engage them in a thoughtful and meaningful conversation. This vignette illustrates the interrelationship of language arts and science in the early childhood classroom.

Connecting Language Arts and Science

Forty-three states currently have early learning standards for prekindergarten with the remaining seven states in progress (Neuman & Roskos, 2005). However, as an increasing number of states implement standards and benchmarks for young children, teachers are often perplexed by the challenge of helping children with varying abilities and backgrounds reach the standards (Hatch, 2002). For example, only Texas (Scott-Little, Kagan, & Stebbins Frelow, 2003) has standards that provide guidance on how to support mastery for second language learners. Likewise, few states provide guidance on how children with disabilities should be included in classroom efforts to move children toward mastery of the standards.

"Language and literacy is the most common domain to be included in early learning standards" (Scott-Little et al., 2003, p. 26), and is often identified as an area that should be prioritized in the teaching of young children (Neuman, Roskos, Vukelich, & Clements, 2003; Ruhland, 2001). Perhaps this is part of the reason that teachers are focused on the planning and implementation of language arts activities in the classroom, and leave "little time for science" (Worth & Grollman, 2003, p. xvi). However, opportunities to explore science concepts through active, hands-on experiences can provide useful contexts for helping children with disabilities, second language learners, as well as typically developing children, move toward mastery of the language and literacy standards in ways that are appropriate for them.

Recent research has demonstrated the importance of unplanned conversations in developing the language skills of young children (Hart & Risley, 1999). Science at the early childhood level has the potential to support language and literacy learning, because it is about "real stuff" (Conezio & French, 2002). Science content gives all young

Science at the early childhood level has the potential to support language and literacy learning, because it is about "real stuff" ....

children something to listen to, and to talk, write, and inquire *about*. It is reasonable to assume that in a classroom where children are active scientific investigators, there will be many opportunities for both teacher-initiated and child-initiated practice and expansion of language and literacy skills. Let's take a closer look at this connection by using the Illinois Early Learning Standards (Illinois State Board of Education, 2002) and benchmarks related to oral language (e.g., listening, speaking, inquiry) to think about how these benchmarks can be achieved through a classroom science curriculum.

Listening, Speaking, and Inquiry

The Illinois Early Learning Standards (Illinois State Board of Education, 2002) include five benchmarks related to listening, speaking, and inquiry:

1. Listen with understanding and respect to directions and conversations.
2. Communicate needs, ideas, and thoughts.
3. Seek answers to questions through active exploration.
4. Relate prior knowledge to new information.
5. Communicate information with others.

Movement toward mastery of these benchmarks increases when teachers take advantage of the opportunities for language development

... [C]hildren are natural-born scientists and investigators ....

inherent in science activities. If educators believe " ... activities that are based on children's interests provide motivation for learning" (Bredekamp, Knuth, Kunesh, & Suylman, 1992, p. 16), then it follows that children are more likely to *listen with understanding* when the topic is real and meaningful to them. The study of science is a way of thinking about and examining things that are part of the children's everyday lives and environment (Conezio & French, 2002). The processes of investigating and discovering why the things in their world work the way they do is engaging and meaningful to most young children. It has often been said that children are natural-born scientists and investigators (Gopnik, 1999).

Preschoolers are naturally curious, and they learn about the world through exploration with their senses and through talk (Wells, 1986). Exploring scientific concepts, such as cause and effect relationships, animate versus inanimate, or changes in properties of matter, captures children's interest and motivates them to communicate their needs, ideas, and thoughts (Conezio & French, 2002). Science experiences in which children seek answers to questions through active exploration help them satisfy this curiosity, generate new questions, and meet their natural drive to make sense of their world. Additionally, in a classroom where curiosity is valued, and where children are encouraged to actively investigate together, a sense of community can be created.

As they observe, hypothesize, predict, and experiment, children's knowledge and understanding of basic concepts grows (Bowman, Donovan, & Burns, 2000). They become more confident in their own abilities and are more likely to communicate their ideas and knowledge to others. They are eager to explore new ideas and relate them to what they already know. Teachers can capitalize on this drive by introducing science concepts and materials in a way that includes all children and leads to ongoing discussion in a variety of conversational settings (e.g., snack time, outdoors, arrival) that occur during daily life in the classroom. Preparing the preschool classroom environment to support ongoing exploration and discussion, and supporting children's emerging language skills through active listening and conversation, are keys to making this happen (Dickinson, 2001a).

The purpose of this article is to provide teachers with information on how to prepare and organize the classroom environment for supporting children's exploration and discussion, and for connecting language and literacy with science. Specifically, guidelines for constructing an area that is rich in literacy and science content, and for introducing a new science theme will be provided and described. First, however, let's return to our opening vignette to understand in more general terms the language/literacy and science connection.

The Language/Literacy and Science Connection

Children learn best about the body of knowledge called science by performing experiments using the scientific method. For example, in Mrs. Amaya's preschool classroom, the children observe that the soles of their shoes light up when they stamp their feet. The explanation of the phenomenon they form is that stamping their feet causes their shoes to light up. When Mrs. Amaya challenges their first hypothesis by pointing out that her shoes do not light up when she stamps, the children propose a new hypothesis: batteries in the toes of some shoes cause them to light up. Mrs. Amaya then challenges the children to think of ways that they might test their hypothesis. She has an opportunity not only to help the children discover the function of batteries, but also to engage them in an investigation that will provide meaningful opportunities for the application of a wide variety of language arts skills. Mrs. Amaya begins this discussion during circle time, and a logical continuation of the topic might unfold during choice time, as follows.

The next day, cutting open a discarded light-up shoe is an activity in the science area during choice time. Mrs. Amaya allows interested children to have a turn sawing at the sole of the shoe with a small saw. After some effort, they discover a tiny, white plastic box inside the sole of the shoe. The children talk excitedly to each other about the size, shape, and possible function of the box. Mrs. Amaya records their comments on a chart displayed in the science area above the dissected shoe. She asks the children how they think a battery works. Once again, she records their predictions. Mrs. Amaya invites the children to go to the school library with her to find books that might explain how batteries work.

The next day, Mrs. Amaya sets out in the science area tools that run on batteries, and she encourages the children to try taking the batteries out and replacing them. As the children experiment with the batteries, they make observations to each other and Mrs. Amaya. At the end of the day, she asks them to share what they found out as they experimented with batteries, flashlights, a radio, and an alarm clock, and she adds their new knowledge to the chart with a different colored marker.

■■■■■■■■■■■■■■■■■■■■ ■

...[W]hen children engage in the process of making observations, generating hypotheses, and planning and carrying out experiments, they often engage in listening, communicating with others, seeking answers through active exploration, and relating prior knowledge to new information.

As illustrated in the vignette, when children engage in the process of making observations, generating hypotheses, and planning and carrying out experiments, they often engage in listening, communicating with others, seeking answers through active exploration, and relating prior knowledge to new information. Discussions about and explorations in science provide an especially useful context for the application of standards identified in the language arts domain. Science and discovery provide children with something meaningful to write, talk, read, and inquire about.

Why Create a Science-Rich Environment?

Most early childhood classrooms provide activity areas, although the variety of these areas differs across classrooms. Most classrooms include a dramatic play or housekeeping area, a book area, an art area with an easel, a block area, a table for sand and water play, an area for floor toys, and an area for manipulatives. The science area, however, is often minimal or nonexistent. If asked for an explanation of this lack, teachers might say something like, "Science happens all over the classroom. Chemistry happens when children mix paint in the art area, physics happens when children build in the block area, and biology happens when children take care of the class pet, so why should a classroom have a science area?" While there is some truth to that justification, teachers who think this way overlook the potential of a well-developed science area to support the development of language and literacy, as well as other skills.

A Science Center

The science area in many classrooms consists of a static set of objects and tools associated with early childhood science learning (e.g., a magnifying glass, a basket of pinecones, a bowl of seashells, magnets) (Conezio & French, 2002). The objects and tools typically change very little throughout the year. Furthermore, teachers often have little idea about what science concepts or skills young children should learn, so they provide materials that they perceive as "typical." Sometimes early educators refer to this type of science area as a classroom "science museum."

Science centers designed to engage young children in discovery and exploration, on the other hand, include materials for experimentation that relate to current classroom discussions; child-friendly and accessible reference materials; and an inviting, comfortable space for exploration and interaction with others. The science center should be a place where children come together to examine and investigate topics. While individual children sometimes visit the science area, it is more likely that children will gravitate there in small groups. Small groups provide an effective context for children to develop and practice oral language (Dickinson, 2001a). Further, children's performance on cognitive tasks has been found to improve as a result of social interaction with more advanced peers (Katz, Evangelou, & Hartman, 1990). When children visit a science center, they often work cooperatively with others as they explore materials in a prepared environment. They acquire an understanding of what they see in this area by discussion with other children and/or the teacher. When children select this area independently, this fact increases the likelihood that they will work productively.

The science center creates an environment that promotes language learning in a social context. Introduction to new materials and experi-

The science center creates an environment that promotes language learning in a social context.

ments in this area also stimulates the acquisition and use of new vocabulary words. For example, Mrs. Amaya might promote the understanding of terms such as: sole, charge, electricity, and current. The addition of new vocabulary words has been linked with cognitive growth (Hart & Risley, 1995) and later academic success (Dickinson, 2001b).

Guidelines for Supporting Language in the Science Center

The preschool teacher should consider the following four basic guidelines for supporting language learning in the science center: (1) selection of high interest materials; (2) appropriate arrangement of the physical environment; (3) engaging children in extended conversations; and (4) modeling the steps of scientific problem solving.

High Interest Materials

Select materials that are high interest and worthy of children's study. These should be safe, and they should lend themselves to use by more than one child at a time. In some cases, it may be important to provide multiple materials. For instance, if children are looking at Monarch caterpillars on milkweed leaves, it will facilitate conversation if each child has a magnifying glass, allowing several children to look at the caterpillars at the same time and share their observations.

Physical Environment

The teacher should arrange the physical environment so that children can easily work together. A table with several chairs will invite children to work and talk together. Display materials that are available for exploration attractively on shelves or on a display table. When there are many small pieces or parts to an activity, display them on a tray with a lip to help children successfully move the materials to an area for exploration.

Extended Conversations

Supporting more complex and interactive conversations can help facilitate the inclusion of all children. Teachers provide this support when they engage children in a sequence of contingent interactions. Each participant's behavior is contingent upon what was said or happened before. This behavior might be verbal, or it might be gestural. The teacher creates contingencies to draw children into the conversation. For example, consider if Mrs. Amaya was conversing with a less skilled child.

Mrs. Amaya: Wow! Look at your shoes! That is so cool. They light up when you step down.

James: (Nods his head).

Mrs. Amaya: How do you make them light up?

James: Do this (jumps up and down).

Mrs. Amaya: Wow! What do you think will happen if I jump up and down?

James: Let's see.

Mrs. Amaya: (Jumps up and down).

James: (Shakes his head back and forth) Nope.

Mrs. Amaya: Any ideas why not?

James: Gots no lights.

Mrs. Amaya: Gee, I sure wish I had lights in my shoes.

In this conversation the child has limited verbal skills, so Mrs. Amaya reduces the distance between her interactions with the child (see Figure 1). She extends the sequence of their interaction by creating contingencies. The early childhood educator adjusts this model to challenge more skilled children by including more children in the conversation and by reducing the number of times he or she joins in the sequence. The educator's goal is to increase the number of contingent child-child interactions, and to reduce parallel monologues. If we continue the conversation in the vignette with the goal of increasing child-child interactions, it might proceed like the following.

Emily: I think we should X-ray them.

Taylor: Yeah. Let's do that.

Dillon: No, you guys! We don't have an X-ray machine.

Mrs. Amaya: Any ideas of what else you could try?

Dillon: Let's cut 'em open.

Emily: Okay!

Dillon: I wonder what we can cut them with.

Emily: Let's cut them open at the workbench, guys!

Taylor: Yeah. Let's get a saw.

Emily: I'll get it.

Dillon: Okay. Taylor, you tighten the vice. I'll saw first.

Mrs. Amaya limited her interactions in this conversation (see Figure 2) because she recognized that the children were creating contingencies for each other.

Figure 1
Conversation Flow for a Less Skilled Child
Mrs. Amaya interacts more frequently and makes contingencies to draw a less skilled child into conversation.

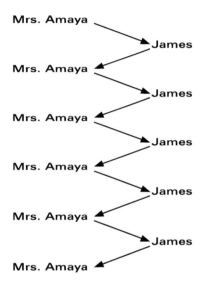

Scientific Problem Solving

As teachers encourage young children to observe, hypothesize, experiment, or to "think like scientists," they support mastery of both science and language arts knowledge and skills, and they strengthen positive dispositions. Modeling is a tool that teachers can use to support children's mastery of these skills and to strengthen dispositions. For example, children are encouraged to pose their own questions or ideas for scientific research when early educators carefully observe children and ask them questions to probe their thinking, or make comments that will help children think more deeply and expand on their investigations (e.g., "What would happen if … "). Modeling new vocabulary words and engaging children in activities in which those words are likely to be used optimizes the teacher's ability to make use of the language arts and science connection in the early childhood classroom.

Figure 2
Conversation Flow for Supporting Peer-to-Peer Interactions
Mrs. Amaya supports child-child conversation by reducing her interactions in the conversation.

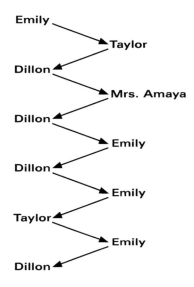

Introducing a New Science Theme

Circle time, the portion of the classroom day when children gather as a whole group, typically takes up about 30% of children's class time (Layzer, Goodson, & Moss, 1993). If these group times are orderly and promote thinking, they can be very beneficial (Dickinson, 2001b). Early childhood educators often introduce new concepts or activities during circle time. If the introduction of new science material is done well, practice in listening and engaging in conversations can be increased. Highlighting examples from the vignette, four guidelines (i.e., select high interest topics, use real objects, allow direct hands-on discovery and investigation, and record children's findings) that can contribute to the successful introduction of a new science theme while supporting the development of language arts skills are described below.

Select High Interest Topics

Selecting a high interest topic of study that is part of the children's own environment and experience and has potential for rich exploration, investigation, and discussion is very important. This topic might be one the teacher identifies by actively listening to children's conversations and watching their play, or it might be a topic that he or she selects independently. In the vignette the topic was light-up shoes, but it could easily have been any number of things that surround children in their everyday lives, such as dirt, worms, cars, plants, insects, water, locks, trees, or food. These are topics that are worthy of children's time and that invite scientific investigation. Topics that do not provide opportunities for first-hand investigation make many topics unsuitable for study (e.g., the geographic location of the school may make some topics less worthy of investigation). For instance, the ocean would not be a good topic for preschoolers in Illinois, but it would be a fine topic for children who live near a coast.

Use Real Objects

It is helpful if the teacher brings an actual object to begin the discussion. For example, Mrs. Amaya wants to continue the investigation of light-up shoes, so she brings a light-up shoe to circle time. When teachers bring something to circle time that is of interest to the children, they can pique their curiosity and begin the process of question and answer, observation, and hypothesis generating that is characteristic of the scientific method. For example, a teacher might bring a faucet to circle time to start a conversation about water, a packet of seeds to start a conversation about gardening, or a steering wheel to start a conversation about cars.

Allow Direct Hands-On Discovery and Investigation

Children develop the habit of careful listening when they have had frequent experiences of their teacher sharing information followed by investigations. When children are asked to participate in activities that revolve around drill of isolated skills or rote learning, such as repeating the days of the week, they are less likely to become engaged in conversation (Dickinson, 2001a; NAEYC, 1998; Wells, 1986). The potential impact of the study of a topic is also reduced when educators demonstrate materials to children, tell them about the materials, and then put the materials away. With pressure to demonstrate children's progress and measure outcomes, teachers are in danger of becoming overly concerned with covering the material, rather than in helping children "uncover the topic." If we give children opportunities to explore through direct, first-hand investigation, children are more likely to become engaged in conversation and discussion.

Teachers who link the discussion at circle time to ongoing investigation that takes place during choice time are more likely to engage children in discussion. For example, in the case of the light-up shoes,

Mrs. Amaya might share the children's earlier conversation about the light inside the shoes, and ask the children for their guesses about how the lights work. She then records all the children's guesses on a dated web chart (Beneke, 1998), without indicating which guess she thinks will be right. She labels the chart "Light-Up Shoes" and tacks the web on the bulletin board, so that she and the children can refer back to it during later discussions. As the children talk about what they know, they discover that they have many experiences in common, as well as unique knowledge and experiences. The teacher can encourage child-child interaction and support children in sharing these discoveries.

Mrs. Amaya then asks the children how they might find out what causes shoes to light up. The children suggest that they can find out by cutting open an old shoe. Mrs. Amaya tells them that she will bring a shoe the next day for them to dissect. She asks the children what they think they will find inside, and records their predictions on a piece of paper to display on the board alongside the web chart. She asks the children to share the basis for their predictions. The next day when the children gather at circle, they discuss what they found inside the shoe and add their new knowledge to the web.

Record Children's Findings

Recording children's findings, as Mrs. Amaya does in the example, conveys teachers' interest in the children's ideas and their respect for the children's work. It communicates the idea that what children do during choice time is important. To provoke further interest, Mrs. Amaya might introduce a new nonfiction book, such as *Batteries, Bulbs, and Wires* (Glover, 2002) to add to the science area and introduce new vocabulary words that relate to pictures in the book. As the children draw more conclusions from their work in the science area, these findings can be added to the web chart. This approach conveys a message that Mrs. Amaya is interested in the children's ideas and that she expects and welcomes their input. As children successfully participate in verbal interactions more frequently, they are motivated to engage in future interactions.

Conclusion

Science activities that are of high interest are likely to engage children who have difficulty focusing or staying on task. Mrs. Amaya helped children move toward mastery of standards in listening, speaking, and inquiry by selecting a meaningful science topic for discussion and study, inviting children's hypotheses, listening to and respecting the children's ideas, encouraging first-hand investigation, and providing the children with opportunities to revisit and summarize their learning. When early childhood educators become active listeners who capitalize on the natural curiosity of young children and their disposition to make sense of their experiences and their world, they can make optimal use of the natural connection between language arts and science in the preschool classroom. This connection is strengthened when teachers introduce more science content and engage children more frequently in interactions and activities about the science content.

Note

You can reach Michaelene M. Ostrosky by e-mail at ostrosky@uiuc.edu

References

Beneke, S. (1998). *Rearview mirror reflections on a preschool car project.* Champaign, IL: Early Childhood and Parenting (ECAP).

Bowman, B. T., Donovan, M. S., & Burns, M. S. (Eds.). (2000). *Eager to learn.* Washington, DC: National Academy Press.

Bredekamp, S., Knuth, R. A., Kunesh, L. G., & Suylman, D. D. (1992). *What does research say about early childhood education?* Oakbrook, IL: North Central Regional Education Laboratory (NCREL).

Conezio, K., & French, L. (2002). Science in the preschool classroom: Capitalizing on children's fascination with the everyday world to foster language and literacy development. *Young Children, 57*(5), 12–18.

Dickinson, D. K. (2001a). Putting the pieces together: Impact of preschool on children's language and literacy development in kindergarten. In D. K. Dickinson & P. O. Tabors (Eds.), *Beginning literacy with language* (pp. 257–287). Baltimore: Paul H. Brookes.

Dickinson, D. K. (2001b). Large group and free-play times: Conversational settings supporting language and literacy development. In D. K. Dickinson & P. O. Tabors (Eds.), *Beginning literacy with language* (pp. 223–255). Baltimore: Paul H. Brookes.

Glover, D. (2002). *Batteries, bulbs, and wires: Young discoverers' science facts and experiments.* New York: Kingfisher Press.

Gopnik, A. (1999). *Scientist in the crib: Minds, brains, and how children learn.* Marietta, GA: Active Parenting Publications.

Hart, B., & Risley, T. (1999). *The social world of learning to talk.* Baltimore: Paul H. Brookes.

Hart, B., & Risley, T. (1995). *Meaningful differences in the everyday experiences of young American children.* Baltimore: Paul H. Brookes.

Hatch, A. J. (2002). Accountability shovedown: Resisting the standards movement in early childhood education. *Phi Delta Kappan, 83,* 457–462.

Illinois State Board of Education, Division of Early Childhood. (2002). *Illinois early learning standards.* Springfield, IL: Author.

Katz, L. G., Evangelou, D., & Hartman, J. A. (1990). *The case for mixed-age grouping in early childhood education.* Washington, DC: National Association for the Education of Young Children (NAEYC).

Layzer, J. I., Goodson, B. D., & Moss, J. (1993). *Life in preschool: Vol. 1. Final report to the U.S. Department of Education.* Cambridge: Abt Associates.

National Association for the Education of Young Children (NAEYC). (1998). Learning to read and write: Developmentally appropriate practices for young children. *Young Children, 53*(4), 30–46.

Neuman, S. B., & Roskos, K. (2005). The state of state prekindergarten standards. *Early Childhood Research Quarterly, 20*(2), 125–145.

Neuman, S. B., Roskos, K., Vukelich, C., & Clements, D. (2003). *The state of state prekindergarten standards in 2003.* Ann Arbor, MI: Center for the Improvement of Early Reading Achievement (CIERA). Retrieved February 27, 2005, from http://www.ciera.org/library/archive/2003–01/.

Ruhland, J. R. (2001, September 4). President's column: Early childhood education should be a national priority. *School Board News.* Retrieved February 26, 2005, from http://www.nsba.org/site/doc_sbn. asp?TRACKID=&VID=58&CID=324&DID=8044.

Scott-Little, C., Kagan, S., & Stebbins Frelow, V. (2003). Creating the conditions for success with early learning standards: Results from a national study of state-level standards for children's learning prior to kindergarten. *Early Childhood Research & Practice, 5*(2), 20. Retrieved February 20, 2005, from http://ecrp.uiuc.edu/v5n2/little.html.

Wells, G. (1986). *The meaning makers: Children learning language and using language to learn.* Portsmouth, NH: Heinemann.

Worth, K., & Grollman, S. (2003). *Worms, shadows, and whirlpools: Science in the early childhood class-room.* Washington, DC: National Association for the Education of Young Children (NAEYC).

Use of Sociodramatic Play to Develop Literacy Skills in Early Childhood Settings

Rashida Banerjee, M.S.Ed., and Eva Horn, Ph.D.,
University of Kansas

our-year old Alexis is busily poring over a piece of paper with a pencil in her hand in the dramatic center. Jerome walks up to her and asks what she is doing. She impatiently says, "Oh, don't bother me. Tomorrow is Mandy's [pointing to her doll] birthday and I'm making my shopping list." "I want to help," Jerome says. Alexis looks up from her paper, thinks for a moment and says, "Okay, you can help me get the things from the store. But first I have to make the list for you." After a few scribbles she hands the paper to Jerome saying, "This is the list of things you need to get from the store, but you have to be fast—there's lots to do." Jerome skips away, list in hand, to the nearby pretend store.

For some time the relationship between play and literacy has interested scholars (e.g., Christensen & Kelly, 2003; Davidson, 1996; Einarsdottir, 1996; Morrow & Rand, 1991; Neuman & Roskos, 1990; Pelligrini & Galda, 1998). A number of studies have been conducted that link play and literacy development in early childhood (e.g., Morrow & Rand, 1991; Neuman & Gallagher, 1994; Neuman & Roskos, 1990; Pelligrini & Galda, 1998; Vedeler, 1997). Roskos and Christie (2004) reviewed articles on the play-literacy interface published between 1992 and 2000. In their critical analysis, they found strong evidence that well designed literacy-promoting play environments provide for language experiences that lead to young children building connections between oral and written modes of expressions and thus support their later literacy learning.

The aim of this article is to serve as a useful guide for early educators in understanding the relationship between literacy and play, particularly sociodramatic play. The article begins by briefly defining play and then more specifically sociodramatic play. These definitions are followed by a discussion of the development of sociodramatic play in young children and its influence on the child's overall development. Next, the integration of early literacy and sociodramatic play with descriptions of the role of the early educator in facilitating the connection for the young child is presented. The article concludes by defining early literacy and providing specific strategies for early educators to use to enhance the environment to facilitate sociodramatic play and incorporate literacy content.

What Is Play?

Often observers of children's activities say that they can reliably recognize play when they see it but find it difficult to define (Linder, 1993). The most commonly agreed upon criterion for the definition of play is that it does not serve an immediate purpose (Pelligrini & Galda, 1998). Children are more concerned with the means than the ends. For example, a little girl moving crayons over a paper may be happy just with the feeling of the crayon in her hand making the strokes, rather than what she is creating on the paper.

In addition to the "means over ends" criterion, researchers have also defined play according to the following attributes: (1) positive affect, (2) active engagement, (3) intrinsic motivation, (4) limited external rules, and (5) nonliterality (Garvey, 1990; Rubin, Fein, & Vanderberg, 1993). The attribute of positive affect or enjoyment can be clearly observed in children's laughter, smiles, singing, and expressions of joy (Schaefer, 1993). Just as do adults, children seek out enjoyable activities and the feeling of pleasure sustains the activity. Children's enjoyment is thus directly linked to the children's active engagement or deep involvement without distraction.

> *Just as do adults, children seek out enjoyable activities and the feeling of pleasure sustains the activity.*

Play fully absorbs children's interest. Closely linked to both enjoyment and engagement is probably the most frequently cited attribute of play, intrinsic motivation (Garvey, 1990). Play is voluntary. Play does not have extrinsic goals, rather motivations are intrinsic and play is enjoyed more for its processes than for its end result. Furthermore, in play children themselves set the rules for defining the roles of players, for entry into the play, for the development of the plot, and generally for acceptable behaviors (Fein, 1981). The final attribute of play, nonliterality, refers to the play vs. reality distinction inherent in pretend or fantasy (Howes, 1992; Singer & Singer, 1990). The pretend play world is a place where children can escape reality, forgo limits, and have control over what they do.

For example, in the opening vignette the children are engaged in play because they choose to play, rather than because it has been suggested to them. Control rests with the two children (one child has a greater level of control than the other) and there is no direct adult intervention in the play. Evidence that the children are creating their own internal reality occurs throughout the play as the planning and "shopping" for the party develop and are enacted.

"Play is practice in choosing, doing, and problem solving" (Jones, 2003 p. 32). As they play children are practicing thinking, innovating, negotiating, and risk-taking skills. They construct their own rules and pace their rate of tackling and learning new tasks. While children initiate and control their own play, adults support both play and the learning that can occur by providing a variety of things to do and carefully observing and providing verbal acknowledgment of the children's actions and words as needed.

What Is Sociodramatic Play?

Imaginative play, symbolic play, dramatic play, and sociodramatic play are a few of the terms that have been used to describe the type of play illustrated in the opening vignette (Pelligrini & Galda, 1998). According to Piaget (1962), different stages of cognitive development are characterized by the different types of play. Piaget's preoperational stage of cognitive development is typified by symbolic play or those activities in which a child uses one thing to represent another. Thus children's initial symbolic representations incorporate object representation, that is, those in which one object is used to represent another (e.g., a block representing a car). Later symbolic play is conducted without the support of objects, such as when Alexis remarks in the opening vignette, "Oh, don't bother me. Tomorrow is Mandy's birthday ...." It is important to note that children's symbolic play is rule-governed, though the rules are established as a part of the play and undergo numerous changes as the play progresses (Pelligrini & Galda, 1998).

Influential psychologist Smilansky (1968) expanded on Piaget's work on play and coined the term *sociodramatic play* to define pretend play in a social context. According to her definition of sociodramatic play six characteristics are involved: (1) make-believing using objects (e.g., using a block of wood as a car); (2) assuming a make-believe role (e.g., pretending to be a dog, a cat, or a teacher); (3) make-believing about a situation or action (e.g., pretending that a box is a house); (4) persisting or being able to continue the play in face of challenges (e.g., in the vignette, instead of being upset by Jerome's intrusion in her play, Alexis finds a way to involve him); (5) using language to communicate the context of play (e.g., a child pretending to be the mother exclaims, "I'm going to the grocery store. I've run out of baby food."); and (6) interacting socially while playing (e.g., in a pretend doctor's office, a child asks her "patient," "How do you feel today?").

According to Smilansky, dramatic play only includes the first four characteristics while sociodramatic play also has the last two characteristics. In sociodramatic play, children do not merely reproduce existing societal scripts; they change them in some very idiosyncratic and creative ways. They often use gestures and language that might be ambiguous in the conveyance of meaning (Singer & Lythcott, 2004). This form of play occurs most frequently during the preschool period and accounts for a significant portion of children's behavior during this period.

The terms *dramatic play* and *sociodramatic play* have been used interchangeably in the literature on play. For the purpose of clarity, the term sociodramatic play is henceforth used in this article to refer to the definition of play described by Smilansky (1968), which incorporates all six characteristics of play.

Development of Sociodramatic Play in the Young Child

As the child develops, so does the quality of the child's play (Davidson, 1996). The play of the two-year old child is relatively simple. The children enact pretend actions, such as feeding or sleeping, but do not have pretend roles. They seem to recognize and enjoy each other's presence but few social interactions occur. The theme of the three-year old child's play typically revolves around the activities and routines of the home and community, and begins to include more details. The three-year old takes on roles, though these roles are fluid and can shift quickly to fit the moment and a number of different themes being enacted in the same space. For example, a child pretends to be Mommy and feeds her doll and, in the next instance, puts on a hat and is ready to go to the office like her father. Language becomes a more important part of three-year old children's play and is used to define their play or to tell each other the roles they have chosen.

The play of the four-year old child becomes more social, and the interaction is maintained for a longer period of time with the children taking an active role in the play (Davidson, 1996). The play themes continue to be familiar ones, but they move beyond just home and school to include scenarios seen on TV, in a restaurant, or at the grocery store, for example. The four-year old child uses less physical activity and more language to set the direction of the play. By the time children are five, they develop detailed fantasy themes in their play involving many actors and often continuing from one day to the next. The five-year old child is easily able to deal with small problems that may arise in their pretend play and still keep the play going. The five-year old child is also able to incorporate more people and more diverse roles into the play.

As children grow and develop, one can see broad variations in individual children's play even within the same age group. Jones and Reynolds (1992) coined the term "master players" to describe children who are " ... skilled at representing their experiences symbolically in self-initiated improvisational drama" (p. 1). Recognition of the importance of understanding individual differences in both areas of strength and areas of need becomes an important role for early educators as they work to support children's play development just as they do across other domains of child development.

Role of Sociodramatic Play in Child Development

While definitions of play include the characteristic of it being purposeless, play is very much considered to serve an important function in the development of the child (Davidson, 1996). Sociodramatic play fosters development in all domains including social-emotional, cognitive, language, and physical development, and allows children to function at their highest level of competence (Vygotsky, 1977).

Social-Emotional Development

In a world where children have very little control, sociodramatic play puts the children in charge (Davidson, 1996). Sociodramatic play allows children to play the roles of the important people in their lives. When children are faced with a problem that they cannot find a way to resolve on their own, adult help may be required. Through sociodramatic play they learn the importance of cooperation, self-control, and conflict management (Thompson, 2004). Children learn to feel good about themselves and also are able to handle fears, anxieties, and other negative emotions. Play has also been shown to contribute to the development of social skills such as turn taking, following rules, empathy, and self-regulation (Howes, 1992).

Cognitive Development

Sociodramatic play allows children to explore their understanding of events, characters, and objects in a manageable context (Pelligrini & Galda, 1998) and encourages thinking and learning in children (Thompson, 2004). The play is by no means static: "Children reenact and adapt their schema, or concepts about the events they are enacting" (Davidson, 1996, p. 6) as they continue to engage in play experiences. Young children imitate other people's actions and explore their environments during their play. Imitation and exploration are the twin sources of early knowledge (Thompson, 2004). As children get older and gather more

Imitation and exploration are the twin sources of early knowledge ....

experiences of daily life, they enact these experiences in their play. For example, one boy chases another around the room, pretending to be his dog chasing the neighbor's dog. As children engage in sociodramatic play they learn to solve problems, negotiate, plan and prepare ahead, and think of new and creative ways to enact their themes.

Language Development

The use of explicit oral language in symbolic play provides children with opportunities to practice and expand their language by adding more sophisticated components, namely narrative structure and linguistic terms that are also fundamental to school-based literacy lessons and reading comprehension (Christensen & Kelly 2003; Pelligrini & Galda, 1998). During sociodramatic play, children interact and use new language as they plan, negotiate, compose, and implement their ideas. In the vignette, as Alexis and Jerome engage in planning for Alexis' doll's birthday, they enact a scene they have witnessed and adapt it to suit their script.

Physical Development

As children pretend, they have ample opportunity to practice their gross and fine motor skills (Garvey, 1990). As they button a shirt to dress a doll, hold a pencil and pretend to make a list of items, or prepare a "meal" in the "kitchen," for example, they are practicing their fine motor skills. While pretending to be a policeman and chasing a thief, they are practicing a number of gross motor skills.

What Is Early Literacy?

The concept of early literacy refers to children's early experiences with reading and writing, which begin to shape their view of print in the home and the neighborhood (Smith, 1989). Early literacy places the onset of literacy shortly after birth. Unlike earlier beliefs that literacy begins in the first grade, becoming literate occupies every waking moment throughout childhood. Because written language is based on spoken language, children's experiences with speech and conversation provide them essential knowledge that supports later reading development (Christensen & Kelly, 2003). Researchers have found that children develop the ability to reflect on and talk about their daily activities and experiences through interactions with family members, teachers, and more competent peers (Hart & Risley, 1999). Reading skill is built on this awareness of spoken language. For example, children learn that words are separate units of spoken language, and this is related to their developing abilities to recognize and write words. Thus reading, writing, and speaking are interrelated (Dickinson, 2001).

There is mounting evidence of a relationship between children's emerging literacy abilities and the emergence of the ability to talk about one's own mental state, about words, and about the difference between the words one utters and the meaning one intends to communicate (Dickinson, 2001; Torrance & Olson, 1985). Though everyday conversations provide children with invaluable opportunities for acquiring language abilities and have social value, only the abilities to reflect on language and communicate novel information are linked to literacy.

Integrating Early Literacy and Sociodramatic Play

Children involved in sociodramatic play demonstrate greater proficiency and interest in reading (Christensen & Kelly, 2003; Einarsdottir, 1996). Preschool children pursue play with literacy material when given the opportunity, particularly older preschool children as they move closer to transitioning to kindergarten/school. Neuman and Roskos (1990), in their study of the impact of specially-designed print environments on children's literacy activities in play, concluded that well planned environmental design changes can allow play to become an important context for reading and writing explorations. Morrow and Rand (1991) also investigated the impact of environmental changes in preschool classrooms and, in addition, examined patterns of teacher guidance on children's literacy behavior. They found that not only was the environment important but that the teacher's role was extremely important in guiding and modeling literacy behavior.

... [W]ell-planned environmental design changes can allow play to become an important context for reading and writing explorations.

Dickinson and Smith (1992), in their study of preschool children, found a strong correlation between kindergarten measures and pretending at age three, but not age four. Younger children are usually not able to enter fully into the relatively adult constructed language environments. However, in pretend play they can control the complexity level and fully exercise their emerging language abilities. Four-year olds, on the other hand, benefit from exposure to challenging adult constructed discourse. Pretending is an ideal area in which children can develop literacy-related language skills. While increased pretend time in preschool classrooms may not lead directly to acquisition of literacy-related skills by the time children transition to kindergarten, pretending is an activity that allows children the opportunity to use and develop important language skills that are linked to early literacy growth (Dickinson, 2001).

Thus there is evidence for supporting two strategies for enhancing language and literacy development in sociodramatic play: (1) adults as mediators/facilitators, and (2) enhancing "language richness" of the environment. The next two sections present a discussion of our current knowledge of the roles of adults and environments in the development of play in children, and specific strategies and tips for early educators based on the research evidence.

Role of the Early Educator

Davidson (1996) discusses four roles of the early educator in supporting young children including observer, stage manager, player, mediator, and interpreter. As an observer, the teacher simultaneously facilitates the children's play, assesses the children's progress, maintains order in the classroom, covers main aspects of the curriculum, helps the children in their specific need areas, and attends to many other crucial aspects of the daily routine (Jones & Reynolds, 1992). Being an observer is one of the most important roles for the early educator. Skill in observation helps the early educator know how to best facilitate children's play, when adult help is required to mediate problems, what intrigues the children, or what part of the play should be extended (Davidson, 1996). Ongoing observations provide a much more adequate sample of behaviors than any test or standardized evaluation tool for young children. They permit focus on children's abilities, not disabilities: what a child can do or does do, rather than what he or she does not do.

Just like the stage manager in a play, the early educator's role as a stage manager is to facilitate children's sociodramatic play (Davidson, 1996). As the stage manager, the teacher ensures that the required props are available to the children and that there is enough, clearly defined space for the children to move around in easily, including for children with adaptive devices such as wheelchairs.

As players or participants early educators can take an active role in the children's play, particularly if the children are having difficulty starting or maintaining play (Christensen & Kelly, 2003). However, teachers need to be able to gauge the need for their interference and only assume a role accordingly.

During any play episode, conflicts are likely to arise between the children. It is at this point that the teacher's role as mediator may come into play. The early educator can serve as mediator if the children are unable to resolve the conflict themselves, and help them learn how to problem solve solutions (Davidson, 1996; Jones & Reynolds, 1992). For example, at the post office center, two children both want to be the cashier and stand at the counter. They begin to bicker. The teacher walks over and directs the attention of the children to the fact that there is a problem that must be resolved. He asks the children for a suggestion about what can be done to solve the problem. One of the children replies that they can take turns. The other child agrees to let her playmate take the first turn while she is the customer. In acting as the mediator, the teacher highlights the positive behavior of the children, ignores the negative behavior (the bickering), withholds judgment about the children, and helps them to dialogue and come to a consensus.

Due to the egocentric nature of children, they are often unable to understand each other's needs and even their own needs (Davidson, 1996). The teacher can assume the role of interpreter and describe children's actions to make them aware of other children. Through questions the early educator can also help children clarify their own play and actions. In the previous example, the two children are both initially interested in what they individually want (i.e., to be the cashier) without concern for what the other wants. Their teacher helps them understand and be aware of the other child's needs through questions. Noninterfering and open questions often help children to clarify their own play.

Adults serve as essential scaffolds by bridging the children's current developmental capabilities to their future language, cognitive, social, and emotional processes.

Adults have important roles to play at different points in children's sociodramatic play. The appropriate role, whether as observer, stage manager, player, mediator, or interpreter, is dependent on the immediate context and the children's level of sophistication with play, communication, and social interaction (Klein, Wirth, & Linas, 2003). Adults serve as essential scaffolds by bridging the children's current developmental capabilities to their future language, cognitive, social, and emotional processes.

Designing Environments to Facilitate Sociodramatic Play

Through carefully designed indoor play environments, the early educator can enhance and extend literacy opportunities for young children and subsequently encourage developmentally appropriate literacy activities and learning (Morrow & Rand, 1991). By providing children with appropriate props, space, time, and guidance, adults can significantly expand the learning opportunities of children during pretend play. In addition to providing rich extended language experiences (e.g., during meal times, book reading, or free times throughout the day), teachers need to provide children time and settings in which they can use language with each other as part of sociodramatic play. Teachers also can help parents realize the important contributions made by home oral language experiences to young children's developing literacy abilities.

An example of an effective pretend play area, which promotes language and literacy, is a kitchen play setting containing cookbooks, recipe cards, coupons, and grocery packages in the cupboards. Other popular items include notepads and pencils that children can use to make endless (indecipherable) lists. Another favorite setting with children is the "office," containing the literacy tools for writing letters, signing "checks," doing homework, and writing plans. Providing a variety of office supplies such as pencils, pens, markers, forms, files, assorted papers, a telephone and telephone book, stickers, stamps, a mailbox, and so forth can make for an exciting setting for children to engage in pretend work and activities.

All literacy supplies should be easily accessible to the children. Literacy-enriched environments can significantly influence the literacy behaviors of children (Neuman & Roskos, 1990). Children often will use literacy objects, such as a book or tablet of paper, in imaginative ways, creating new uses for them as tools and furthering their play (e.g., changing a newspaper page into a treasure map). Their literacy-related play will likely become increasingly longer in duration and more complex as they participate more frequently in sociodramatic play episodes.

Literacy materials must be available to engage children in literacy activities. Older children in preschools benefit from working with print (Einarsdottir, 1996). Teachers should enrich their sociodramatic play areas with literacy props and integrate print into the curriculum. Presenting print in connection with sociodramatic play is not only a natural extension of children's preschool work, but also gives the children an opportunity to work with challenging and stimulating situations.

Merely having print present in the environment does not ensure that children will pay attention to the print (Morrow & Rand, 1991). Children need strategies to interact with print and derive meaning from it. Using a calendar for birthdays, having the children's names on their cubbies for keeping their things or labeling the items in the room are some of the ways that teachers can encourage children to learn to read. Poems, songs, and favorite stories with pictures can be printed on a chart board for children to read with adults or on their own.

It is important to note that teachers may need to make some modifications, adaptations, and accommodations to their classroom environments, activities, materials, adult roles, and their expectations of children's behaviors in order to include children with special needs and enhance their participation in play (Sandall et al., 2002). For example, a child may need to carry a picture book with her to different centers to communicate with her peers, or another child may need an adult to help him break down tasks into smaller steps so that he can participate in the play. Sandall and her colleagues provide multiple examples of concrete adaptations and modifications that can be made in preschool classrooms to support children with disabilities to access and engage with the materials and activities of the preschool classroom.

Conclusion

Children with disabilities are often at risk for communication and language delays—crucial elements in the foundation of early literacy skills (Hart & Risley, 1999). It has been suggested that since the sociodramatic play of the young child is child-centered, child-selected, and child-directed, that for children with language impairments or developmental delays this type of play is particularly important as it motivates the children to stretch their skills in order to keep the play going (Davidson, 1996; Pelligrini & Galda, 1998; Sandall et al., 2002). The teachers of young children need to see literacy growth as multifaceted: requiring growth in oral discourse skills as well as print-related abilities, occurring through interactions with peers as well as adults, and the growth of print and language skills occurring in the home as well as in preschools and other schools. It is the responsibility of the teacher and the preschool program to build a connection between home and school, particularly with children whose homes may provide few literacy materials and activities. Building continuity between home and school ensures that literacy developed in school can be meaningfully applied to the larger context of the child's community.

Note

You can reach Rashida Banerjee by e-mail at rbanerjee@ku.edu

References

Christensen, A., & Kelly, K. (2003). No time for play: Throwing the baby out with the bath water. *Reading Teacher, 56,* 528–530.

Davidson, J. (1996). *Emergent literacy and dramatic play in early childhood education.* Albany, NY: Delmar.

Dickinson, D. K. (2001). Putting the pieces together: Impact of preschool on children's language and literacy development in kindergarten. In D. K. Dickinson & P. O. Tabors (Eds.), *Beginning literacy with language* (pp. 257–287). Baltimore: Paul H. Brookes.

Dickinson, D., & Smith, M. (1992, December). Preschool contributions to early language and literacy development. Paper presented at the (42nd) annual meeting of the National Reading Conference, San Antonio, TX.

Einarsdottir, J. (1996). Dramatic play and print (preschools in Iceland combine dramatic play with learning activities). *Childhood Education, 73,* 352–357.

Fein, G. (1981). Pretend play in childhood: An integrative review. *Child Development, 53,* 1095–1118.

Garvey, C. (1990). *Play.* Cambridge: Harvard University Press.

Hart, B., & Risley, T. (1999). *The social world of learning to talk.* Baltimore: Paul H. Brookes.

Howes, C. (1992). *The collaborative construction of pretend: Social pretend play functions.* Albany, NY: State University of New York Press.

Jones, E. (2003). Playing to get smart. *Young Children, 58*(3), 32–37.

Jones, E., & Reynolds, G. (1992). *The play's the thing: Teachers' roles in children's play.* New York: Teachers College Press.

Klein, T., Wirth, D., & Linas, K. (2003). Play: Children's context for development. *Young Children, 58*(3), 38–45.

Linder, T. (1993). *Transdisciplinary play-based intervention: Guidelines for developing a meaningful curriculum for young children.* Baltimore: Paul H. Brookes.

Morrow, L. M., & Rand, M. (1991). Promoting literacy during play by designing early childhood classroom environments. *Reading Teacher, 44,* 396–402.

Neuman, S., & Gallagher, P. (1994). Joining together in literacy learning: Teenage mothers and children. *Reading Research Quarterly, 29,* 382–401.

Neuman, S., & Roskos, K. (1990). Play, print, and purpose: Enriching play environments for literacy development. *The Reading Teacher, 44,* 214- 222.

Pelligrini, A., & Galda, L. (1998). *The development of school-based literacy: A social ecological perspective.* New York: Routledge.

Piaget, J. (1962). *Play, dreams, and imitation in childhood.* New York: Routledge.

Roskos, K., & Christie, J. (2004). Examining the play-literacy interface: A critical review and future directions. In E. Zigler, D. Singer, & S. Bishop-Joseph (Eds.), *Children's play: The roots of reading* (pp. 21–38). Washington, DC: Zero to Three Press.

Rubin, K. B., Fein, G. G., & Vanderberg, B. (1993). Play. In E. M. Hetherington (Ed.), *Socialization, personality, and social development* (pp. 693–774). New York: Wiley.

Sandall, S., Schwartz, I., Joseph, G., Horn, E., Lieber, J., Wolery, R., & Odom, S. (2002). *Building blocks for teaching preschoolers with special needs.* Baltimore: Paul H. Brookes.

Schaefer, C. E. (1993). *The therapeutic powers of play.* Northvale, NJ: Jason Aronston.

Singer, J., & Lythcott, M. (2004). Fostering school achievements and creativity through sociodramatic play in the classroom. In E. Zigler, D. Singer, & S. Bishop-Joseph (Eds.), *Children's play: The roots of reading* (pp. 36–54). Washington, DC: Zero to Three Press.

Singer, D. G., & Singer, J. L. (1990). The house of make-believe: Children's play and the developing imagination. Cambridge: Harvard University Press.

Smilansky, S. (1968). *The effects of sociodramatic play on disadvantaged preschool children.* New York: Wiley.

Smith, C. (1989). Emergent literacy: An environmental concept. *Reading Teacher, 42,* 528–534.

Thompson, R. (2004). Development in first years of life. In E. Zigler, D. Singer, & S. Bishop-Joseph (Eds.), *Children's play: The roots of reading* (pp. 54–66). Washington, DC: Zero to Three Press.

Torrance, D., & Olson, N. (1985). *Language, literacy, and mental states.* Chicago: Spencer Foundation.

Vedeler, L. (1997). Dramatic play: A format for "literate" language? *British Journal of Educational Psychology, 67,* 153–167.

Vygotsky, L. (1977). Play and its role in the mental development of the child. In M. Cole (Ed.), *Soviet developmental psychology* (pp. 76–99). White Plains, NY: M. E. Sharpe.

Resources

Within Reason

Supporting Early Development in Young Children

Camille Catlett, M.A., and Pamela Winton, Ph.D.,
University of North Carolina at Chapel Hill

Patsy L. Pierce, Ph.D.,
Raleigh, NC

Sarah E. Hamel, B.A.,
University of North Carolina at Chapel Hill

A place to discover good, inexpensive materials for providing effective services to very young children and their families

Each issue will review resources that cost $50 or less on a different aspect of early intervention. This issue features resources that help teachers and other adults create literacy-rich environments.

Creating a Classroom Literacy Environment
by Children's Literacy Initiative (2002)

Designed for child care, Head Start, and prekindergarten teachers, this 47-page guide provides specific suggestions for ways to make a classroom a literacy-rich environment. It covers topics such as room arrangement, centers, reading aloud, extending books into activities, and developing phonemic awareness. More than 50 color photographs are included illustrating how to implement these various elements of a literacy-rich classroom environment.

> Children's Literacy Initiative
> 2314 Market Street
> Philadelphia, PA 19103
> (215) 561-4676
> http://www.clionthewer.org/

Environmental Print in the Classroom: Meaningful Connections for Learning to Read
by Jennifer Prior and Maureen R. Gerard (2004)

One main component of literacy-rich environments is environmental print. This book offers practical suggestions for incorporating environmental print into preschool classrooms and using this print to help children learn to read. Suggestions are also provided to help parents use environmental print when teaching their children to read.

International Reading Association
800 Barksdale Road
P.O. Box 8139
Newark, DE 19714-8139
(800) 336-7323
http://www.reading.org

Creating Literacy-Rich Homes

This "Reading is Fundamental" Web site begins by describing the importance of having a home that is literacy-rich. Articles on diverse topics (e.g., building a family library, developing a reading environment, creating a literacy-rich home) are available to download. Activities that can promote a literacy-rich home environment and additional Web resources are also provided.

http://www.rif.org/parents/literacyrich/default.mspx

Talking & Reading Together

Looking for excellent information to share with families? This Web site from PBS Parents provides easy-to-read information on how children become readers and writers and provides tips and suggestion for how family members can help their children develop by talking, reading, and writing together every day. A section called "Pick an Age" provides age-by-age (e.g., baby, toddler, preschooler) information on "how children develop" and "what parents can do."

http://www.pbs.org/parents/issuesadvice/talkingandreading/

Preschool Literacy Web Home Page

Visit this Web site from the University of Connecticut's Literacy Web to access a variety of literacy resources, "visit" preschool classrooms around the world, and see how other children are applying their literacy skills. Applications are included for children who are culturally-, linguistically- and ability-diverse.

http://www.literacy.uconn.edu/pkhome.htm

Literacy Work Stations: Making Centers Work
by Debbie Diller (2003)

This book, filled with photos of classrooms, offers practical suggestions for more than a dozen literacy workstations including big book, writing, drama, ABC, and poetry. Suggestions are provided on how to set up the stations and what materials to include. Materials are available in both English and Spanish.

Stenhouse Publishers
P.O. Box 11020
Portland, ME 04104-7020
(800) 988-9812
http://www.stenhouse.com/

Early Language and Literacy Classroom Observation (ELLCO) Toolkit/User's Guide
by Miriam W. Smith and David K. Dickinson (2002)

A field-tested toolkit designed for pre-K through third grade classrooms, this assessment includes a "Literacy Environment Checklist," a "Classroom Observation and Teacher Interview," and a "Literacy Activities Rating Scale." These three components allow teachers to gain a better understanding of how their classroom promotes literacy.

Paul H. Brookes
P.O. Box 10624
Baltimore, MD 21285-0624
(800) 988-9812
http://www.brookespublishing.com/

What to Look for in a Quality Literacy-Rich Preschool Classroom

Looking for ways to turn existing classroom centers into literacy-rich centers? This resource from the North Carolina State Improvement Project (http://www.ncsip.org) may be for you! In addition to providing many suggestions on incorporating literacy into every part of a preschool classroom, this document describes nine key elements to look for in literacy-rich environments.

http://www.ncsip.org/LiteracyRichClassroom.pdf

Kansas Kids Ready for Learning!

Recognizing and responding to emergent and early literacy as a critical link in providing quality early childhood experiences, the Kansas State Board of Education (KSBE), in collaboration with the Kansas State Department of Education (KSDE) and Kansas Inservice Training System (KITS), developed this useful Web site. Subtitled *Links to Early*

Literacy for Families and Providers, this site "links" Internet users with quality early literacy Web sites and initiatives within the state of Kansas and across the nation. Developed for use by parents and early childhood providers, this Web site has sections addressing play and young children, reading to young children, language development and young children, writing and young children, learning to read, math and young children, frequently asked questions, and resources. Each of these sections is divided into "What We Know," "Activities," and "Special Needs" for ease of use.

http://www.readyforlearning.net/

DEC Recommended Practices

A Comprehensive Guide For Practical Application in Early Intervention/Early Childhood Special Education
(second printing)

Bridging the gap between research and practice, the book *DEC Recommended Practices* provides guidance on effective practices for working with young children with disabilities. The recommended practices are based on a review and synthesis of the research literature and the practices identified as critical by various stakeholders in early intervention/early childhood special education.

The book contains recommended practices in the following areas:

- Assessment—*John Neisworth and Stephen Bagnato*
- Child-focused interventions—*Mark Wolery*
- Family-based practices—*Carol Trivette and Carl Dunst*
- Interdisciplinary models—*R.A. McWilliam*
- Technology applications—*Kathleen Stremel*
- Policies, procedures, and systems change—*Gloria Harbin and Christine Salisbury*
- Personnel preparation—*Patricia Miller and Vicki Stayton*

The second printing of *DEC Recommended Practices* is easier to use than ever and has been completely updated with additional resources and advice, program checklists for both parents and administrators, and two new chapters dealing with the real-life experiences of users. Put *DEC Recommended Practices* to work for your students today!

Visit our website to view companion pieces to this text, read about other exciting and useful products or to place an order. Click on the 'Store' tab.

Division for Early Childhood (DEC)
www.dec-sped.org

DEC
Recommended Practices

Selected Strategies for Teaching Young Children With Special Needs

This product, available in both DVD and VHS, demonstrates environments and several teaching proceedures from *DEC Recommended Practices: A Comprehencive Guide for Practical Application in Early Intervention/Early Childhood Special Education* (Sandall, Hemmeter, Smith and McLean), including:

- Peer-mediated strategies
- Using consequences
- Prompting strategies
- Naturalistic teaching procedures
- Environments that promote learning

These effective strategies are based on an extensive literature review and focus groups of parents, teachers, and administrators about what promotes learning for young children with special needs.

Visit our website to view companion pieces to this **DVD/Video**, read about other exciting and useful products or to place an order. Click on the 'Store' tab.

Division for Early Childhood (DEC)
www.dec-sped.org